Think Like a Shark

Other Books by Jim Toomey

Sherman's Lagoon: Ate That, What's Next?
Poodle: The Other White Meat
An Illustrated Guide to Shark Etiquette
Another Day in Paradise
Greetings from Sherman's Lagoon
Surf's Up!
The Shark Diaries
Catch of the Day
A Day at the Beach
Surfer Safari
Planet of the Hairless Beach Apes
Yarns & Shanties (and Other Nautical Baloney)
Sharks Just Wanna Have Fun
Discover Your Inner Hermit Crab
Confessions of a Swinging Single Sea Turtle
Never Bite Anything That Bites Back

Treasuries

Sherman's Lagoon 1991 to 2001:
Greatest Hits and Near Misses
In Shark Years I'm Dead: Sherman's Lagoon Turns Fifteen

Think Like a Shark

Avoiding a Porpoise-Driven Life

The Seventeenth SHERMAN'S LAGOON Collection

by Jim Toomey

Andrews McMeel Publishing, LLC

Kansas City • Sydney • London

Sherman's Lagoon is syndicated internationally by King Features Syndicate, Inc. For information, write King Features Syndicate, Inc., 300 West Fifty-Seventh Street, New York, NY 10019.

Andrews McMeel Publishing, LLC
an Andrews McMeel Universal company
1130 Walnut Street, Kansas City, Missouri 64106

www.andrewsmcmeel.com

13 14 15 16 SHO 10 9 8 7 6 5 4 3 2

ISBN: 978-1-4494-2404-6

Library of Congress Control Number: 2012936740

Sherman's Lagoon may be viewed on the Internet at
www.shermanslagoon.com

"If no mistake have you made, yet losing you are . . .
a different game you should play."

—Yoda

YOU LOOK TROUBLED, HAWTHORNE.
OH, THE RESPONSIBILITIES OF BEING MAYOR...
MAYOR

THE LAGOON WAS AWARDED A BIG GRANT FOR A PUBLIC ART PROJECT.
MAYOR

MAYOR

CAN'T FIGURE OUT HOW TO SCAM IT FOR YOURSELF?
I MUST BE LOSING IT IF I CAN'T CHEAT A BUNCH OF ARTISTS.
MAYOR

I JUST HEARD THE WONDERFUL NEWS! WE GOT GRANT MONEY FOR THE ARTS!
HUH? OH, YEAH.
MAYOR

HERE'S SOME MONEY. GO MAKE A SCULPTURE OR SOMETHING. THE BEST ARTIST WINS A PRIZE.

PRIZE? ARTISTS DON'T COMPETE FOR PRIZES. ART IS ABOUT THE SOUL.
MAYOR

THEN GIMME THE MONEY BACK.
I'LL SQUASH THE OTHERS LIKE BUGS.
MAYOR

HI. I'D LIKE SOME GRANT MONEY FOR A SCULPTURE.
YOU?
MAYOR

YEAH. WHY NOT ME?
I DUNNO. I NEVER FIGURED YOU FOR AN ARTSY, RIGHT-BRAINED KIND OF GUY.

DO YOU THINK I'M DRIVEN MORE BY MY RIGHT BRAIN OR MY LEFT BRAIN?
I'D SAY YOU'RE IN NEUTRAL.

HERE YOU GO, BOYS. INVITATIONS TO THE UNVEILING OF MY NEW SCULPTURE.

AS THE LAGOON'S MOST RENOWNED ARTIST, I REALIZE EVERYONE'S WAITING TO SEE **MY** ENTRY.

SO I THOUGHT I'D MAKE AN EVENT OUT OF IT. REALLY DRAW A CROWD.

YOU'RE THE CROWD?
I WAS TOLD THERE'D BE SHRIMP.

THANKS FOR COMING TO THE UNVEILING OF MY SCULPTURE, EVERYONE.

I'M CONFIDENT MY SCULPTURE WILL WIN, AND IT WILL BECOME A CULTURAL CENTERPIECE OF OUR LAGOON...

LADIES AND GENTLEMEN, I GIVE YOU... "MONOLITH FOR THE COMMON MAN."

SHOULD'VE CALLED IT "PORT-O-POTTY FOR THE COMMON MAN."
DOES IT WORK? I GOTTA GO.

NICE TO SEE YOU IN THE SCULPTURE CONTEST, MEGAN.
YOU NEEDED A FEMALE PERSPECTIVE.

MY SCULPTURE MAKES A STATEMENT ABOUT WOMEN'S RIGHTS, BUT IT'S SUBTLE.

YOU MEAN, YOU'RE NOT HITTING PEOPLE OVER THE HEAD WITH IT...

ACTUALLY, IF YOU STAND RIGHT HERE, IT WILL HIT YOU OVER THE HEAD.
NO THANKS.

SHERMAN'S LAGOON

WHEN IT COMES RIGHT DOWN TO IT, I DON'T SEE MUCH OF A DIFFERENCE BETWEEN TURTLES AND CRABS.

TURTLES ARE REPTILES. CRABS ARE CRUSTACEANS.

FURTHERMORE, TURTLES ARE ROUND AND SMOOTH. CRABS ARE POINTY AND SHARP.

TURTLES THINK ABOUT WHAT THEY HAVE. THEREFORE, THEY ARE HAPPY.

CRABS THINK ABOUT WHAT THEY DON'T HAVE. THAT MAKES THEM CRABBY.

TURTLES REPRESENT SWEETNESS AND LIGHT, AND ALL THAT IS GOOD IN THE WORLD.

CRABS REPRESENT DARKNESS AND PAIN, AND ALL THAT IS BAD.

THAT'S THE DIFFERENCE BETWEEN TURTLES AND CRABS.
BESIDES THAT.

OKAY, JUDGING COMMITTEE, WHICH SCULPTURE WON?
NONE OF THESE.

WE'RE GOING WITH THE ONE UP ON THE BEACH.
WHAT ONE ON THE BEACH?

IT'S BRILLIANT. SO LIFELIKE, YOU'D SWEAR IT WAS ALIVE!
OH...

WHY IS THERE A RIBBON ON MY NOSE?
MAYBE YOU'RE ACCESORIZING IN YOUR SLEEP.

WHAT'S UP WITH ALL THE SAILBOATS?

IT'S A REGATTA.

REGATTA? YUM!

IT'S A BOAT RACE.
DANG. SOUNDS LIKE A PASTA.

SO, YOU'RE INTO THIS SAILBOAT RACE THING?
REGATTA.

IT'S ELEGANCE AND BEAUTY... HARNESSING NATURE'S FORCES WITH FINELY TUNED EQUIPMENT TO COMPETE MANO A MANO.

PLUS, YOU'RE TAKING ACTION ON THE RACE.
YEAH. MOSTLY THAT.
BETS TAKEN HERE

I'D LIKE TO PLACE A BET ON A BOAT IN TODAY'S REGATTA.
WHICH ONE?
BETS TAKEN HERE

THE... UH... ONE WITH THE PURPLISH PINK SAIL.
FUSCHIA.
YEAH.
WHY DIDN'T YOU JUST SAY THAT?

DOESN'T SOUND VERY... YOU KNOW... MANLY.
BETS TAKEN HERE

WHAT ABOUT THE FUSCHIA MAN-PURSE? IS THAT MANLY?
JUST MAKE THE BET!
BETS TAKEN HERE

I'D LIKE TO PLACE A BET ON A SAILBOAT IN TODAY'S FRITATTA.
REGATTA.
WHATEVER.

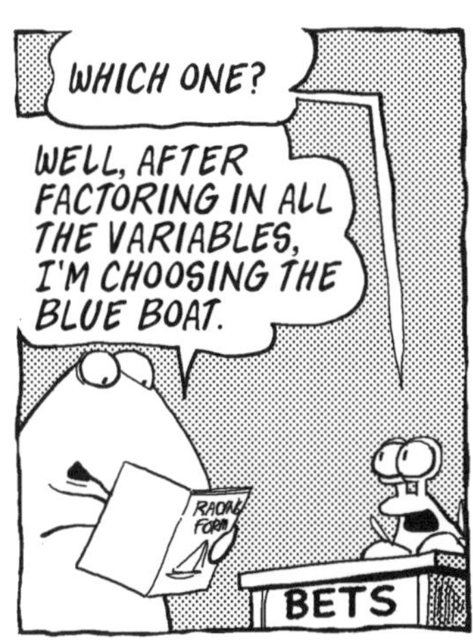
WHICH ONE?
WELL, AFTER FACTORING IN ALL THE VARIABLES, I'M CHOOSING THE BLUE BOAT.
BETS

UH HUH. AND WHAT EXACTLY WERE ALL THESE "VARIABLES"?
SAIL CONFIGURATION, CREW EXPERIENCE, WIND CONDITIONS...

BUT MOSTLY BECAUSE THE CREW IS WEARING MATCHING "KISS MY AFT" TEE SHIRTS.
ALL THE GOOD ONES DO.
RACING FORM

I'D LIKE TO BET ON A BOAT IN THE UPCOMING RACE.
ERNEST, YOU'RE UNDER AGE. I CAN'T TAKE YOUR MONEY.

UNLESS, OF COURSE, YOU WERE TO SHOW ME A REALISTIC-LOOKING FAKE I.D. ...
BETS TAKEN

OH... LIKE, SAY, THIS ONE?

OKAY, SIR GAGA, EVERYTHING SEEMS TO BE IN ORDER.
ALL OF IT ON RED TO WIN.
BETS TAKEN HERE

SHERMAN'S
LAGOON

DO YOU KNOW WHAT YOU LOOK LIKE WHEN YOU SWIM AROUND?

THIS IS YOU:
"DUHHH! DUHHH! I'M A DORKY SHARK...

"I HAVE A BOOGER IN MY NOSE AND I DON'T EVEN KNOW IT! DUHH!"

DON'T YOU DARE DROP THAT BOOGER ON MY DOORSTEP! GROSS! THAT'S JUST PLAIN GROSS!

"I'M A CRAB. I HIDE IN MY CRAB HOLE ALL DAY. WATCH OUT OR I'LL PINCH YOU. DUHH."

HELLO.
HI.

YOU'RE NOT REALLY A CRAB, ARE YOU?
NO.

THAT'S NOT REALLY A SHARK BOOGER, IS IT?
I'M AFRAID SO.

HERE IT COMES! THIS SAILBOAT RACE IS COMING DOWN TO THE WIRE!
GO, BLUE!
C'MON, RED!

TOO CLOSE TO CALL!
PHOTO FINISH!
WHO WON?

THE **ORANGE** BOAT?
ORANGE? DID ANYONE BET ON ORANGE?
WHO TAKES HOME ALL THAT CASH?

GOLD-PLATED BLENDER, HUH?
AND A LIME MASSAGER.

HAWTHORNE, HAVE YOU EVER SEEN A SHARK DANCE? CHECK OUT MY "FUNKY CHICKEN."

OH MY GOSH! THAT'S FABULOUS! I HAVEN'T SEEN THE "FUNKY CHICKEN" PERFORMED IN AGES!

I'M A PRODUCER FOR "DANCING WITH SHARKS," THE HIT T.V. SHOW. WHAT OTHER DANCES CAN YOU DO?
ALL MY DANCES ARE ROBOT- OR FOWL-RELATED.

SHOW HIM THE "GRUMPY CHICKEN."
I'LL HAVE TO GET INTO CHARACTER.

YOU GOT PICKED FOR THE T.V. SHOW "DANCING WITH THE SHARKS"?
YEAH.

I WAS JUST MESSING AROUND AND SOME PRODUCER SAW ME.

BUT YOU DANCE LIKE FRANKENSTEIN.

YOU'RE GOING TO TOTALLY EMBARRASS YOURSELF ON NATIONAL T.V.
INTERNATIONAL.

DO YOU REALIZE THAT ONE OF MY DREAMS IS TO APPEAR ON THE T.V. SHOW "DANCING WITH THE SHARKS"?

IF YOU CAN DO IT, I CAN DO IT. I'M GOING TO PRACTICE AND TRY OUT.

IF THAT'S YOUR DREAM, MEGAN, THEN I'M GOING TO SUPPORT YOU THE BEST WAY I POSSIBLY CAN...

...FROM TWO MILES AWAY ON THE GOLF COURSE.
THAT MEANS A LOT.

FILLMORE! WHAT ARE **YOU** DOING HERE?
AUDITIONING.

BUT THIS T.V. SHOW IS CALLED "DANCING WITH THE **SHARKS**." YOU'RE NOT A SHARK.
I KNOW. AND IT'S BLATANT DESCRIMINATION!

THIS IS COMPLETELY UNFAIR! I DEMAND AN AUDITION!
SECURITY!!
AUDITIONS
Dancing with the Sharks

PERHAPS INSTEAD OF DANCING WITH THE SHARKS, YOU'D PREFER SLEEPING WITH THE FISHES.
DO YOU AT LEAST VALIDATE?

NAME, PLEASE.
MEGAN.
AUDITIONS
Dancing with the Sharks

SO, TELL ME, MEGAN, WHY ARE YOU RIGHT FOR "DANCING WITH THE SHARKS"?
JUST LOOK AT THIS BODY. I'M A NATURAL-BORN DANCER.

AUDITIONS
Dancing with the Sharks

DO YOU KEEP THE DANCER'S BODY INSIDE OF **THIS** ONE?
AM I IN OR NOT?

by Jim Toomey

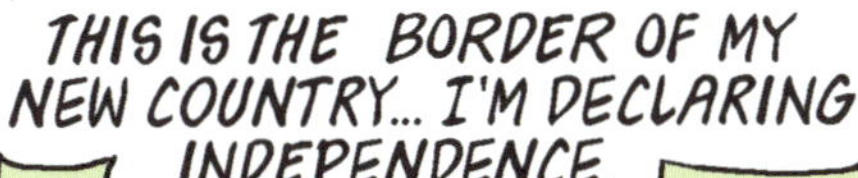
THIS IS THE BORDER OF MY NEW COUNTRY... I'M DECLARING INDEPENDENCE.

LET'S SEE... WHAT SHOULD I CALL MY NEW COUNTRY?

"CRABLAND"
NAH. SOUNDS LIKE A THEME PARK.

"CRUSTACEA"... YEAH.

"THE DEMOCRATIC REPUBLIC OF CRUSTACEA." EVEN BETTER.

NOW WE NEED A FLAG ... IT'LL BE ORANGE, WITH THE IMAGE OF AN OPEN CLAW, THE CRAB SYMBOL OF PEACE AND FELLOWSHIP.

OUR NATIONAL ANTHEM:
HAIL CRUSTACEA! CRUSTACEA MY FAIR LAND...

CURRENCY: THE CRUSTI.
PRINCIPAL EXPORT: BALONEY.

LOOKS LIKE WE'RE BOTH GOING TO BE CONTESTANTS ON "DANCING WITH THE SHARKS."
YEP.

YOU REALIZE THAT THIS HAS BEEN A LIFELONG DREAM OF MINE. AND YOU'RE HERE BECAUSE OF A TOTAL FLUKE.
YES.

SO, YOU DO YOUR THING AND I'LL DO MINE. MAY THE BEST SHARK WIN. GOT IT?
GOT IT.

SHERMAN, YOU'LL BE PARTNERED WITH SIMONE.
OKAY, YOUR THING JUST BECAME MINE.
RIGHT.

"DANCING WITH THE SHARKS" IS STARTING. CHANNEL 4.

THERE'S SHERMAN!
BOY, HE LOOKS NERVOUS.

AND YOU KNOW WHAT HE DOES WHEN HE GETS NERVOUS...

THINK THOSE BUBBLES ARE GOING TO COST HIM?
THE JUDGES DON'T LIKE IT.

WELL, SO MUCH FOR MY DREAM OF WINNING "DANCING WITH THE SHARKS."

WE GOT ELIMINATED IN THE FIRST ROUND!
MEGAN, YOU KNEW I WAS A BAD DANCER WHEN YOU MARRIED ME.

SEE? I PUT "BAD DANCER" ON MY PRENUPTIAL DISCLOSURE OF THINGS I'M BAD AT.

THAT THING IS A FIRE HAZARD. WHY DIDN'T YOU GIVE ME A SPREADSHEET?
BAD AT COMPUTERS.

GO AHEAD AND TEE OFF. I NEED TO USE THE BOYS' ROOM.
10TH HOLE

DANG.

I ALWAYS FORGET. ARE WE SQUIDS OR STARFISH?
SQUIDS.

MEN'S ROOM OUT OF ORDER?! YOU GOTTA BE KIDDING ME!
OUT OF ORDER

I REALLY NEED TO GO.
OUT OF ORDER

I SEE YOU'RE DOING THE POTTY DANCE.

YOU WANT ME TO CLAP ALONG?
I DON'T SEE THAT HELPING ANY.

I JUST USED THE LADIES' ROOM 'CUZ THE MEN'S ROOM IS OUT OF ORDER...

YOU GOTTA CHECK IT OUT. IT'S UNBELIEVABLE!

OH, GOODNESS! THEIR TOILET PAPER IS TRIPLE PLY! AND QUILTED!

WHAT'S IN THE MEN'S ROOM?
20 GRIT.

SHERMAN'S
LAGOON

WHO ORDERED THE GIANT SQUID?
I DID.

YOUR FORK, MONSIEUR.

BON APPETIT!
GRRRRRRRR

AAUUUGH!

OOF!

OW! UGH! AUGH!

CAN I HAVE A BITE?
FEEL FREE TO BITE IT ALL YOU WANT, MEGAN!

COME ON! YOU GUYS HAVE TO SEE THE REST OF THE LAGOON LADIES' ROOM!
WELL, OKAY.

WHOA! THEY EVEN HAVE MUZAK!
IN SURROUND SOUND.

ACTUALLY...

...IT'S A STRING QUARTET IN STALL FOUR.
HELLO.

BOY, I AM NEVER GOING BACK TO THE LAGOON MEN'S ROOM.
I HEAR YA.

THIS LADIES' ROOM GOES ON FOREVER.
HEY, AN ELEVATOR!

LET'S SEE WHAT'S ON THE SECOND FLOOR.

GIFT SHOP.
GUYS! OVER HERE! IT'S A FONDUE STATION!

GUESS WHERE I WAS TODAY, MEGAN.
THE GOLF COURSE.

YES. AND HAWTHORNE HAD TO USE THE BOYS' ROOM... BUT IT WAS OUT OF ORDER.
FASCINATING.

SO, HE USED THE LADIES' ROOM...
HE WENT IN?

YES. IT'S NOT AT ALL LIKE THE MEN'S ROOM. IT'S LIKE SOME SECRET UTOPIAN PARADISE.
HE ENTERED "SHANGRI-LOO"?

I GUESS I'LL HAVE TO KEEP USING THE LADIES' ROOM AS LONG AS THE MEN'S ROOM IS CLOSED.

MEGAN? IS THAT YOU IN THE STALL NEXT TO ME, GIRLFRIEND?
HAWTHORNE!?

THEY'VE **GOT** TO FIX THE MEN'S ROOM. THIS IS A NIGHMARE!

SO, WHAT HAPPENS NOW? WE GOSSIP WHILE WE TAKE CARE OF BUSINESS?
AAUUGH!! IT GETS WORSE!

WHERE DO YOU THINK **YOU'RE** GOING?
THE BATHROOM.

THE MEN'S ROOM IS BACK IN SERVICE. THE PLUMBER FINALLY CAME AND FIXED IT.

SO, FROM NOW ON, IT'S LADIES ONLY IN THE LADIES' ROOM!

BUT I'M STILL WORKING ON A FILTHY LIMERICK IN STALL THREE.
THE WORLD WILL HAVE TO WAIT.

HMMM, THAT'S INTERESTING.
INTERESTING IN WHAT WAY?

HUH?
IS IT INTERESTING IN A SCIENTIFIC WAY?

...OR INTERESTING IN A "CHARLIE SHEEN IS IN TROUBLE AGAIN" KIND OF WAY?

WHICH WAY WILL END THIS CONVERSATION?
END IT IN AN IMMEDIATE WAY, OR A LINGERING WAY?

Sherman's Lagoon
Wall
Info
Photos

HOW DOES FACEBOOK WORK, HAWTHORNE? I FEEL LIKE I'M IN THE DARK.
DO YOU HAVE ANY FRIENDS?

REAL FRIENDS OR FACEBOOK FRIENDS?
EITHER. YOU GOTTA HAVE FRIENDS.

I'LL FRIEND YOU. NOW I CAN WRITE ON YOUR WALL.
HUH?
HEY! DON'T DO THAT!

AND POKE YOU!
OW!

HOW DO YOU LIKE IT SO FAR?
I DON'T!

WELL, YOU CAN'T UN-LIKE IT UNLESS YOU LIKED IT IN THE FIRST PLACE.
HUH?

SMILE. THERE. GOT A PICTURE OF US, FRIEND.
CLICK!

NOW I TAG YOU!
AUGH! UN-FRIEND! UN-FRIEND!

HERE. SIGN THIS.
SURE.

EXACTLY WHAT AM I SIGNING?
IT'S A PERMISSION SLIP FROM SCHOOL.

IT SAYS YOU'RE A RESPONSIBLE ADULT, AND YOU'RE GOING TO CHAPERONE MY TRIP TO THE NORTH SEA.

YOU PROBABLY SHOULDN'T HAVE WRITTEN "BON JOVI RULES" BY YOUR NAME.
BUT THEY DO.

SO, WHY ARE WE GOING TO THE NORTH SEA?
TO STUDY COLD WATER CORAL.

YOU WON'T HAVE A LOT OF FAT TOURISTS FROLICKING IN THE SURF UP THERE, SHERM. IT'S STRICTLY A SEAFOOD DIET.

ONE MORE BEFORE WE HIT THE ROAD.
A LITTLE ONE.

HERE WE ARE IN THE NORTH SEA.
AND IT'S COLD.

CHECK IT OUT! LOPHELIA CORAL!
OH, RIGHT. WE CAME ALL THIS WAY TO LOOK AT CORAL.

YOU KNOW, CORAL IS AN ANIMAL. MAYBE THERE'S A WAY TO COMMUNICATE WITH IT.

HELLO? HELLO? WHICH WAY TO THE MEN'S ROOM?
NICE OPENER.

CHECK IT OUT. MUST BE SOME KIND OF CRAB.
CARRIER CRAB, PAL.

WHAT ARE YOU A CARRIER OF? TYPHOID?
HEY, YOU'RE **FUNNY**!

I'M ACTUALLY A "CARRIER" OF A BLACK BELT IN KUNG FU, JUDO, JUJITSU AND KARATE.
HOOO HA!

IS THAT ALL YOU GOT?
NEXT, YOU PICK ME UP SO I CAN DISMANTLE YOU.

I THINK I HAVE ENOUGH TO DO MY SCHOOL REPORT ON COLD WATER CORAL.

GOOD. LET'S GO HOME NOW. IT'S COLD HERE.

FISH AREN'T SUPPOSED TO GET COLD.

FISH AREN'T SUPPOSED TO TALK EITHER.
GOT A POINT.

YA KNOW, MEGAN, THAT LAMP REALLY DOESN'T WORK WITH THIS ROOM.
I KNOW.

I'VE BEEN TELLING SHERMAN THAT FOR YEARS, BUT HE WON'T LISTEN.

MAYBE HE'LL LISTEN TO YOU. YOU SEEM TO HAVE A KNACK FOR THAT SORT OF THING.

INTERIOR DESIGN?
CRITICISM.

SHERMAN'S
LAGOON
$1.00

WE NEED TO FIND A WAY TO GET RICH RICH RICH.
WE'RE NOT GETTIN' ANY YOUNGER.

I LIKE YOUR IDEA OF SELLING EVERYONE IN CHINA SOMETHING FOR A DOLLAR.

THAT WOULD MAKE US 1.3 BILLION DOLLARS.
BUT WHAT?
SELL THEM A ROCK.

WHY WOULD EVERYONE IN CHINA BUY A ROCK FOR A DOLLAR?
WE'LL MARKET IT AS A COMMUNICATION DEVICE.

A WIRELESS, HANDHELD COMMUNICATION DEVICE.

EVERYONE IN CHINA CARRIES ONE OF THESE IN THEIR POCKET. AND WHEN THEY DON'T LIKE SOMETHING, THEY THROW THEIR ROCK AT IT.

OKAY. I'LL BE YOUR FIRST CUSTOMER. HERE'S A BUCK.
AND HERE'S YOUR ROCK.

WHAT A STUPID IDEA!
OW!

SHERMAN, YOU'RE BACK. HOW WAS THE NORTH SEA?
COLD.

WHILE YOU'VE BEEN GONE, HAWTHORNE HAS BEEN GIVING ME ADVICE ON REDECORATING.

HAWTHORNE IS GIVING YOU ADVICE?

HE'S NOT CHARGING YOU FOR IT?
I LET HIM STEAL AN ASHTRAY.

WHAT OTHER CHANGES WOULD YOU MAKE IN HERE, HAWTHORNE?
WELL, THIS THROW RUG IS...

HEY, WAIT A MINUTE. ARE YOU TRYING TO GET GET MY INTERIOR DESIGN BUSINESS FOR FREE?

YOU DON'T **HAVE** AN INTERIOR DESIGN BUSINESS!
$ $ $ $ $

HE DOES NOW.
LET'S SEE... I'LL NEED AN ASCOT...

"INTERIORS BY HAWTHORNE"?
YEP.
Interiors by Hawthorne

THIS IS YOUR LATEST VENTURE? WHAT IS IT, EXACTLY?
I COME TO YOUR HOUSE AND POINT OUT THE FLAWS IN YOUR DECOR.

HOW DOES THIS DIFFER FROM ANY OTHER VISIT YOU MAKE?
THIS TIME I CHARGE YOU.

AND, SINCE YOU'RE A CLIENT, I WON'T POINT OUT OTHER FLAWS IN YOUR PATHETIC LIFE.
A BARGAIN AT ANY PRICE.

OKAY, MR. INTERIOR DESIGNER, WORK YOUR MAGIC.
RIGHT...

I'M THINKING WE CHANGE EVERYTHING! BOLD NEW COLORS, CONTEMPORARY FURNITURE.
OOOH! SOUNDS EXCITING!

SOUNDS PRICEY.

I CAN **NOT** WORK WITH HIS NEGATIVE ENERGY!
YOU PICK **NOW** TO HAVE ENERGY?

WELL, HOW DO YOU LIKE YOUR NEWLY DECORATED HOME?
SO AVANT GARDE.

WHAT'S THIS SUPPOSED TO BE? A LAMP?
COOL, HUH?

IT'S ALL THE RAGE IN EUROPE.

SO WAS THE PLAGUE.
YOUR BILL WOULDN'T FIT IN ONE BOX.

DON'T YOU JUST LOVE HOW HAWTHORNE DECORATED OUR PLACE?
NO! IT'S WEIRD!

THIS IS NOT A NORMAL COUCH. IT'S ALL POINTY.

AND THIS LAMP... HOW DO YOU EVEN TURN IT ON?
I THINK IT'S ART.

AND WHERE'S MY FOOTBALL PHONE?
IT WENT DEEP.

SHERMAN'S LAGOON
PLAN "A"
by Hawthorne

HELLO, FILLMORE. HOW'S THE DAY GOING? STILL ON PLAN "A"?
HUH?

PLAN "A." THE PLAN WHERE EVERYTHING GOES RIGHT. YOU GET EVERYTHING DONE; YOU CHECK ALL THE BOXES.

UNFORTUNATELY FOR MOST OF US, PLAN "A" LASTS ABOUT FIVE MINUTES.

WE'RE ALL RUNNING AROUND EXECUTING PLAN "B." LIFE IS ONE BIG PLAN "B."

I DON'T HAVE A PLAN "A" OR A PLAN "B." I ASSESS WHATEVER LIFE BRINGS ME AND I REACT ACCORDINGLY.

OH, I SEE. YOU LIVE IN THE MOMENT.
SAD.

LOOKS LIKE LIFE HAS BROUGHT ME AN ANNOYING CRAB.
SHOULD'VE PLANNED FOR IT.

OKAY, I WAS SKEPTICAL, BUT I SAW WHAT YOU DID FOR SHERMAN AND MEGAN...
Interiors by Hawthorne

AND I'D LIKE TO HIRE YOU AS MY INTERIOR DESIGNER.
UM...

PROBLEM?

I DON'T HAVE TO GO INSIDE THAT SHELL, DO I?
NO ONE GETS IN THE MAN CAVE.

FILLMORE, WHEN I DESIGNED YOUR PLACE I WANTED IT TO HAVE A TROPICAL FEEL.
OKAY.
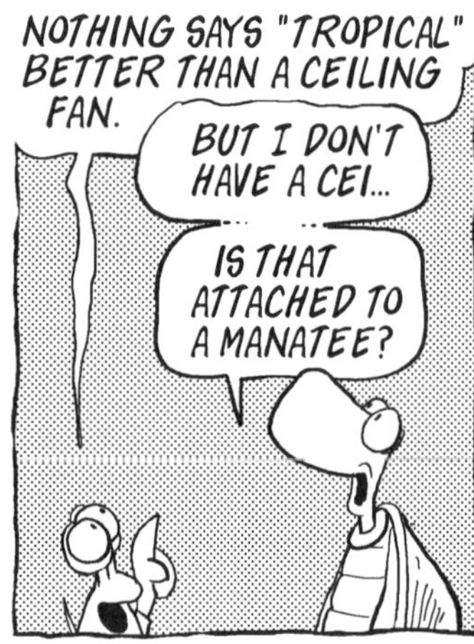
NOTHING SAYS "TROPICAL" BETTER THAN A CEILING FAN.
BUT I DON'T HAVE A CEI...
IS THAT ATTACHED TO A MANATEE?

YES. THEY DON'T MOVE MUCH.
WHASSUP?

SO, DO I HAVE TO FEED MY CEILING FAN?
SOUNDS WEIRD WHEN YOU SAY IT OUT LOUD LIKE THAT.

AS YOUR INTERIOR DESIGNER, I'M RECOMMENDING A BIG MODERN PAINTING HERE.

THIS ARTIST IS FAMOUS FOR HIS DRIPS AND SPATTERS. IT'S YOURS FOR ONLY $5,000.
OKAY. IF YOU INSIST.

THEY'RE VERY NICE SPATTERS.
OBVIOUSLY A PROFESSIONAL.

SOLD ANOTHER ONE OF YOUR PAINTINGS.

I SAW THE PAINTING YOU PUT IN SHERMAN'S PLACE. I WANT ONE!
Interiors by Hawthorne

THE DRIP-AND-SPATTER TECHNIQUE IS PURE GENIUS. ABSTRACT EXPRESSIONISM AT ITS BEST.

I'LL APPROACH THE ARTIST AND SEE IF HE'S INSPIRED TO PRODUCE ANOTHER.

IT DOESN'T HELP IF YOU WATCH!
JUST MAKE IT HAPPEN.

HAWTHORNE, THAT FANCY HIGH-PRICED MODERN PAINTING YOU SOLD US IS NOTHING BUT BIRD POOP ON A CANVAS!
Interiors by Hawthorne

WHAT IS ART? IT'S SOMETHING THAT EVOKES EMOTION, IS IT NOT?

YOUR STRONG EMOTIONS ARE MERELY PROOF THAT "BIRD POOP ON A CANVAS" IS INDEED ART.

HOW ABOUT "CRAB IN A BLENDER"?
ART?
FEEL THE EMOTION?
I FEEL IT.

FILLMORE, I HEAR YOU'VE GIVEN UP DATING.
YEP.

GIVEN UP ALL HOPE OF FINDING THAT SPECIAL SHE-TURTLE, HUH?
YEP.

YOU'VE CONCLUDED THAT YOU'RE INCOMPATIBLE WITH EVERY FEMALE ON THE PLANET.
YEP.

YOU CAN SPARE ME THE CONSOLING PEP TALK.
WHAT TOOK YOU SO LONG?

SHERMAN'S
LAGOON

YOU KNOW, BEING A SEA SLUG IS COMPLICATED.
REALLY? HOW SO?

JUST LOOK AT ME! I'VE GOT THINGS STICKING OUT EVERYWHERE, AND I'M ALL KINDS OF CRAZY COLORS...

DID YOU KNOW THAT SEA SLUGS ARE NEITHER MALE NOR FEMALE... WE'RE BOTH!

IMAGINE WHAT I GO THROUGH EVERYDAY... WHAT TO WEAR, WHAT TO WATCH ON T.V. ... SHOULD I BUY FLOWERS FOR MYSELF OR NOT?

YOU'RE RIGHT. IT SEEMS VERY COMPLICATED.
BUT THAT'S OKAY.

I'M NOT SO COMPLICATED.
THAT'S OKAY TOO.

SO, YOU'VE GIVEN UP ON DATING, HUH?
YEP.

DARWIN HAD A THEORY ABOUT ANIMALS WHO COULDN'T FIND MATES...

THE SAD. THE PATHETIC. THE SOCIALLY AWKWARD. THE UNPRETTY.

YOU CAN LEAVE NOW.
THE UNNECESSARILY BOSSY.

WELL, I'M OFF TO ACENSION ISLAND FOR THE ANNUAL SWINGING SINGLE SEA TURTLE JAMBOREE. FAREWELL.

I THOUGHT YOU GAVE UP DATING.
I'M GOING AS AN OBSERVER, TO MAKE SURE THE TURTLE MATING SEASON IS DONE PROPERLY.

THAT'S WHAT HAPPENS WHEN YOU CAN'T PLAY THE GAME.
YOU BECOME A REFEREE.

THAT WAS A PRETTY BAD STORM LAST NIGHT. I'M GONNA GO OVER AND CHECK ON KAHUNA.

KAHUNA! ARE YOU OKAY? YOU GOT TOPPLED OVER BY THE STORM!
HUH?

KAHUNA NOT FALL. KAHUNA NOT AWAKE YET.
WEIRD. I'VE NEVER SEEN YOU SLEEP BEFORE...

BOXERS, HUH?
IS THERE REASON FOR SHARK VISIT?

CHECK OUT WHAT THE STORM BLEW IN, KAHUNA. A STATUE, JUST LIKE YOU.

NOT JUST ANY STATUE. IT ANCIENT GODDESS OF LOVE, APHRODITE.

BEEN YEARS SINCE KAHUNA BEEN ON DATE WITH CUTE STATUE... LAST ONE WAS GLORIA.
GLORIA...

WASN'T SHE A CRASH TEST DUMMY?
YEAH. AFRAID TO GET IN CAR WITH HER.

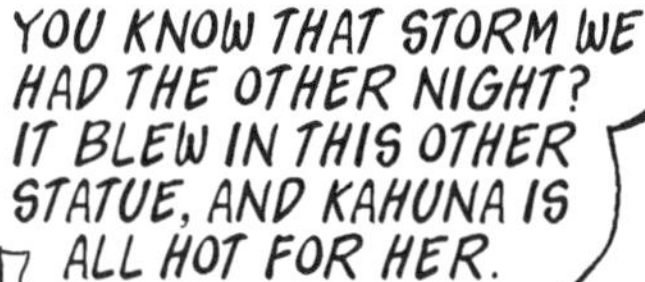
YOU KNOW THAT STORM WE HAD THE OTHER NIGHT? IT BLEW IN THIS OTHER STATUE, AND KAHUNA IS ALL HOT FOR HER.

A STATUE OF WHO?
I'LL GIVE YOU A HINT... ANCIENT GODDESS OF LOVE...

GIMME ANOTHER HINT.
UH... SHE HAS AN AFRO... SORT OF.

WHEN YOU SAY "ANCIENT," DO YOU MEAN, LIKE, EARLIER THAN THE SEVENTIES?
APHRODITE.

SO, KAHUNA, HAVE YOU GOTTEN UP THE NERVE TO TALK TO THAT NEW STATUE...

...APHRODITE, THE GODDESS OF LOVE?
APHRODITE ONE SMOKIN' HOT HUNK OF ALABASTER.

NO...
KAHUNA SHY.

AND THAT GRANITE BREATH ISN'T GOING TO GET YOU ANYWHERE EITHER.
DOESN'T SHARK HAVE HOME?

SHERMAN'S

I JUST ATE A BIG FAT WALRUS!
YOUR DOCTOR TOLD YOU TO LAY OFF THE WALRUSES!

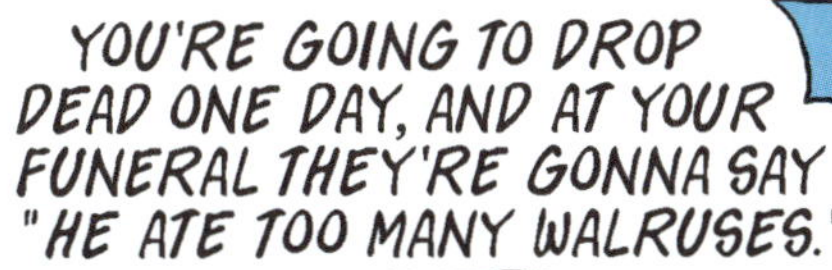
YOU'RE GOING TO DROP DEAD ONE DAY, AND AT YOUR FUNERAL THEY'RE GONNA SAY "HE ATE TOO MANY WALRUSES."

OH, PHOOEY!

NOT ME. I WON'T EVEN BE THERE.

HUH? YOU WOULDN'T EVEN COME TO MY FUNERAL? WHY NOT?
WE'RE NOT THAT CLOSE.

WHADDAYA MEAN "WE'RE NOT THAT CLOSE"? I THOUGHT WE WERE BEST FRIENDS!
OKAY, FINE. I'LL GO.

THEN I'LL SAY, "HE WAS AN OVERLY SENSITIVE AND INSECURE SHARK...

... AND HE ATE TOO MANY WALRUSES."

MAYBE I DON'T WANT YOU AT MY FUNERAL.
MAKE UP YOUR MIND!

HOW'S IT GOING WITH THE NEW STATUE?
NOT GOING.

SHE SEEM LIKE REGULAR STATUE. SHE NOT TALK.

DUDE...

...YOU JUST FOUND THE PERFECT GIRLFRIEND.
HERE COME EAVESDROPPING WIFE WITH WEAPON-LIKE OBJECT.

HI. MY NAME KAHUNA.
HI. I'M APHRODITE.

ME STATUE, YOU STATUE.
YEAH, I NOTICED.

ME **BOY** STATUE, YOU **GIRL** STATUE.

DO YOU ALWAYS HIT ON WOMEN LIKE A TON OF GRANITE?
I **AM** TON OF GRANITE.

FILLMORE, YOU'RE BACK FROM THE ASCENSION ISLAND SWINGING SINGLE SEA TURTLE JAMBOREE... SO SOON!
I MISSED IT!

THEY PUT SOME ANNOUNCEMENT ON FACEBOOK THAT IT WAS RESCHEDULED.

I NEVER FOUND OUT. I DON'T DO FACEBOOK...
I GUESS I SHOULD LEARN.

WHAT DO I NEED TO DO FACEBOOK? A NEW COMPUTER?
AND A NEW FACE.

HEY! THERE'S THE HAPPY COUPLE.

KAHUNA! WHAT DID WE DISCUSS ABOUT THIS ONE?
CAN NO LONGER HANG OUT WITH TURTLE. SORRY.

APHRODITE FIND YOU POMPOUS, DEPRESSING, SELF PITYING, CONDESCENDING.

IS THAT ALL, DEAR?
WEIRD LOOKING, SMELLY.
YOU HAD ME AT POMPOUS.

HEY, KAHUNA, WHERE'S YOUR GIRLFRIEND?
WASN'T WORKING OUT.

KAHUNA ZAP HER INTO LIFELESS STATUE.
OH, I'M SORRY.

THEN HAD HER BUBBLE-WRAPPED, CRATED UP AND SENT TO MUSEUM.
BOY...

... WHEN YOU BREAK UP WITH SOMEBODY, YOU REALLY...
MUSEUM ON MARS.

AWFULLY FAR FROM BAYSIDE LAGOON, AREN'T YOU, BRUNO?
HELLO, SHERMAN.

I'M IN THE MIDDLE OF A PAINTBALL BATTLE. IT'S A MACHO THING.

YOU WOULDN'T QUITE UNDERSTAND.
OH YEAH?

I COULD NOT QUITE UNDERSTAND THINGS BETTER THAN YOU ALL DAY!
SNAPPY COMEBACK.

SHERMAN'S LAGOON

BABYSITTER'S HERE.
TELL HER TO COME IN.

HELLO, ASHLEY. THANKS FOR COMING OVER.

SINCE THIS IS THE FIRST TIME BABYSITTING FOR US, LET ME GO OVER THE ROUTINE.

DINNER, BRUSH TEETH, READ A STORY, LIGHTS OUT AT 8:30. NO T.V. GOT IT?
GOT IT.

I PUT DINNER IN THE OVEN. IT SHOULD BE READY IN 20 MINUTES.

YOU HAVE MY CELL NUMBER IF YOU NEED ME. SEEYA LATER.

YOU'RE STAYING HERE?
WHAT'S FOR DINNER?

WHATCHA GOT THERE, FAT BOY?
A CHALLENGE.

BRUNO AND THE GUYS FROM BAYSIDE LAGOON HAVE CHALLENGED US TO A PAINTBALL BATTLE.
BATTLE!
WUSSIES!

I'M IN! I LOVE THAT STUFF! WE'LL KICK BAYSIDE BUTT!
WHO CAN WE GET FOR OUR THIRD MAN?

FILLMORE, WE NEED YOUR HELP. CAN YOU PRETEND TO BE A MAN FOR A WHILE?
IS THIS ABOUT ARMPIT NOISES AGAIN?

MEGAN, I'M OFF TO A PAINTBALL BATTLE WITH BAYSIDE LAGOON.
HAVE FUN.

FUN? MEGAN, THIS IS ABOUT DEFENDING OUR FAMILY HONOR.

WHERE IS OUR FAMILY HONOR?
IT MIGHT'VE ACCIDENTALLY GONE OUT WITH THE TRASH.

WE'RE HERE, BRUNO. READY FOR PAINTBALL.

I DIDN'T THINK YOU'D SHOW UP.

DIDN'T THINK WE HAD THE GUTS?

DIDN'T THINK YOU COULD FIND THE PLACE.
GOOGLE MAPS. 20 MINUTES.

OKAY, AS CAPTAIN OF THIS PLATOON, YOU NEED TO FOLLOW MY EVERY COMMAND.

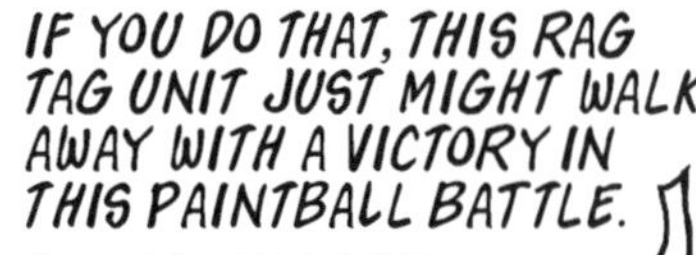
IF YOU DO THAT, THIS RAG TAG UNIT JUST MIGHT WALK AWAY WITH A VICTORY IN THIS PAINTBALL BATTLE.

ANY QUESTIONS?

WHEN DID **YOU** BECOME CAPTAIN?
PANEL ONE. PAY ATTENTION.

OKAY, YOU GUYS OVER THERE ON THE OTHER SIDE OF THIS PAINTBALL CONFLICT...

WHAT SAY WE ALL HUDDLE TOGETHER AND ASK FOR GOOD SPORTSMANSHIP AND SAFETY FOR EVERYONE, FRIEND AND FOE?

ZIP
SPLAT!
ZIP
SPLAT!
ZIP
SPLAT!
ZING!
ZING!
SPLAT!
ZING

THEY DON'T SEEM TO BE THE HUDDLING KIND.
GOOD. I THOUGHT I WAS GONNA HAVE TO FAKE IT.

SPLAT!
ZING!

THIS IS MY FAVORITE PART OF PAINTBALL... THE DEATH SCENE.

I'VE BEEN HIT! HELP!
I'M FADING!
UGH!

I NEED A SOUNDTRACK! VIOLINS!
I'VE GOT LIGHT ROCK. NO VIOLINS.

SHERMAN'S LAGOON

SO, SHERM, TELL ME ABOUT THIS "SIXTH SENSE" YOU SHARKS HAVE.

WE CAN DETECT THINGS... THINGS VERY FAR AWAY.

IT'S MORE OF A TALENT, REALLY. SOME SHARKS ARE BETTER AT IT THAN OTHERS.
DETECT SOMETHING.

LET'S SEE... THERE'S A WOUNDED ANIMAL 16.7 MILES THATAWAY...

AMAZING. NOW YOU GO EAT IT?
YEAH, IF I FELT LIKE IT.

5 MILES IS ABOUT MY LIMIT FOR WOUNDED ANIMALS.

YOU'D BE BETTER OFF IF YOU EITHER HAD LESS TALENT OR MORE MOTIVATION.
I KNOW. IT'S A CURSE!

WELL, WE LOST HAWTHORNE, BUT WE CAN WIN THIS PAINTBALL BATTLE

WE JUST NEED TO WORK AS A TEAM. EVERY ACTION IS CRUCIAL.
OOH! WHAT'S THIS?

SPLAT!
ZING!
SPLAT!
ZING!
SPLAT!
ZING!
SPLAT!
ZING!

WAS LOSING ME WORTH A QUARTER?
LEMME CHECK THE DATE ON IT.

WELL, GUYS, WE'RE COMPLETELY OUTNUMBERED IN THIS PAINTBALL BATTLE.
ZING!
ZING!
OH, DEAR!

OKAY, CALM DOWN...
I THINK IT'S TIME WE SURRENDERED.
ZING!
ZING!
SPLAT!

DID ANYONE BRING A WHITE FLAG?
NO?
ZING!
ZING!
ZING!
ZING!
SPLAT!

FILLMORE, YOU ALWAYS BRING A CHANGE OF UNDERWEAR TO THESE THINGS.
IN MY BACKPACK!
ZING!
ZING!

AS LONG AS WE'RE IN THE VICINITY OF BERMUDA, WE MIGHT AS WELL CHECK OUT THE SARGASSO SEA.

WHAT'S ALL THIS... STUFF... FLOATING AROUND OUT HERE?

THAT'S SARGASSUM WEED. THE LOCALS DEPEND ON IT FOR FOOD...

...AND MEDICINAL PURPOSES.
PEACE.

WHY IS THERE SO MUCH STUFF FLOATING AROUND IN THE SARGASSO SEA, ANYWAYS?

THIS PLACE IS LIKE A GIANT WHIRLPOOL. STUFF DRIFTS IN FROM ALL OVER.

PLASTIC BOTTLES, PLASTIC BAGS...

SIX-PACK HOLDERS.

WHOA! AN OCTOPUS!
YEP. OCTOPUSES LIVE IN THE SARGASSO SEA.

DO YOU SAY "OCTOPUSES" OR "OCTOPI"?
I BELIEVE IT'S "OCTOPUSES."

I ALWAYS THOUGHT IT WAS "OCTOPI."

SHOOT. NOW I WANT EIGHT PIES.
YOU ALWAYS WANT EIGHT PIES.

HEY, ERNEST, I MADE ANOTHER COOL SARGASSO SEA DISCOVERY.
YEAH?

THIS PLACE IS FULL OF SURPRISES... I'LL GIVE YOU A HINT....

WHAT'S LARGE, HAIRY, AND MYSTERIOUS?
THAT RECURRING MOLE OF YOURS?

AUGH!! BIGFOOT!!
HE'S A LITTLE TIRED OF THAT GREETING.

SHERMAN'S LAGOON

ONLY ONE TOURIST ON THE BEACH TODAY, AND HE'S NOT GETTING IN THE WATER.

NO PROBLEM. I CAN WAIT.

WHAT ARE YOU LISTENING TO?
REGGAE.

YOU HAVE TO MATCH THE MUSIC WITH THE MOMENT.

THE SUN IS SHINING, THE WATER'S WARM, AND THE PALM TREES ARE SWAYING IN THE BREEZE.
IT'S A REGGAE MOMENT.

HE JUST GOT IN THE WATER. LET'S GO.
SWITCHING TO "JAWS" THEME.

HEY, I'M THINKING ABOUT DOING THAT.
DOING WHAT?

YOU KNOW. ART.
OH, REALLY...

I SAW THIS GUY ON THE BEACH MAKING PRETTY GOOD MONEY AT IT.
ART IS DONE FOR LOVE.

I LOVE "PRETTY GOOD MONEY."
I WILL **NOT** WELCOME YOU TO THE COMMUNITY.

OKAY, LET'S DO IT. DRAW MY CARICATURE.
COOL. MY FIRST CUSTOMER.
Caricatures $5

OKAY, TELL ME ABOUT YOUR INTERESTS SO I CAN DRAW THE REAL YOU.
WELL, I LIKE TO READ... I LIKE TO WRITE POETRY... I'M A VIRGO...

OKAY, YOU CAN SHUT UP NOW.
GOT ENOUGH TO GO ON?

FORGOT HOW GRATING YOUR VOICE WAS.
NOT THOROUGHLY ENJOYING THIS SO FAR.

HEY, WHAT'S THIS?
Caricatures $5

I DRAW CARICATURES. ONLY FIVE BUCKS.
COOL.
Caricatures $5

SIT DOWN AND LET ME MAKE YOU LOOK STUPID.

THAT'S WHAT MY WIFE SAYS BEFORE WE PLAY SCRABBLE.
THERAPY IS AN EXTRA FIVE BUCKS.

IS MY CARICATURE DONE YET?
YEP.
Caricatures $5

WHAT DO YOU THINK?
GRRRRR...

WHAM!

I SUFFER FOR MY ART.
WE ALL DO.

HOW'S MY CARICATURE COMING?
ALL DONE, SIR.

I THINK I REALLY CAPTURED YOUR SECOND AND THIRD CHIN.

WHAM!

TIP JAR STILL EMPTY?
NOPE. LOOKS LIKE HE SPIT IN IT.

DID YOU CLOSE DOWN THE CARICATURE BUSINESS?
YEAH. TOO DIFFICULT.

EVERYONE TOOK MY INSULTING DRAWINGS SO PERSONALLY.

I'M GOING BACK TO WHAT I DO BEST.

INSULTING WITH WORDS?
YOU GOT IT, BIG NOSE.

SHERMAN'S
LAGOON

AUGH! SHARK!

HEY... AREN'T YOU ALLOWED ONE PHONE CALL BEFORE YOU GET EATEN BY A SHARK?
UM... I GUESS SO.

HI, HONEY, I WON'T BE COMING HOME TONIGHT. I'M GETTING EATEN BY A SHARK.

LOVE YOU, TOO. BYE.

I THINK YOU'RE ALLOWED ONE TWEET AS WELL.
GO AHEAD.

AND ONE BLOG UPDATE, IF I'M NOT MISTAKEN.
FINE.

QUICK PHOTO OF US FOR MY FACEBOOK PAGE.
LET'S GET ON WITH THIS.

WELL, I CAN'T BELIEVE WE ACTUALLY SAW BIGFOOT HERE IN THE SARGASSO SEA.

THIS PLACE IS LIKE A GIANT VORTEX THAT PULLS MYSTERIOUS THINGS FROM ALL OVER.

SHERMAN? IS THAT YOU?
HEY, IT'S...

NESSIE!
DID YOU LADS SEE A TITLEIST VORTEX ITS WAY IN HERE?

CHECK OUT THE ANGLERFISH, SHERM.

HE'S SPECIALLY ADAPTED TO HIDE IN THE SEAWEED HERE IN THE SARGASSO SEA.

WOW. SO, YOU'RE A FISH DISGUISED TO LOOK LIKE VEGETABLE MATTER.
CORRECT.

AND YOU MUST BE VEGETABLE MATTER DISGUISED TO LOOK LIKE A FISH.
THEY'RE KNOWN FOR THEIR SASS.

EELS MIGRATE TO THE SARGASSO SEA FROM ALL OVER EUROPE AND AMERICA.

HELLO. WHERE'D YOU COME FROM?
SOME RIVER IN CROATIA. I CAN'T PRONOUNCE THE NAME.

DON'T SPEAK CROATIAN.
I CAN SHOW YOU HOW IT'S SPELLED...
THERE.

TRY TO PRONOUNCE THAT WORD.
NOKIA.

BABY SEA TURTLES COME TO THE SARGASSO SEA FROM ALL OVER.

THEY HIDE IN THE SEAWEED UNTIL THEY'RE BIG ENOUGH TO FEND FOR THEMSELVES.

LOOK AT THE CUTE LITTLE GUY.

OUCH!
POW!
THAT ONE'S READY.

THE SARGASSO SEA IS AN AMAZING PLACE, SHERM. IT'S LIKE A FLOATING RAINFOREST. I COULD EXPLORE THIS PLACE FOR WEEKS.

BUT IT'S PROBABLY TIME TO HEAD HOME. I DON'T LIKE TO BE AWAY FROM MEGAN TOO LONG.

DOESN'T ABSENCE MAKES THE HEART GROW FONDER?

ABSENCE MAKES THE WIFE GO OUT AND BUY UGLY FURNITURE.

THE BEACH APES ARE HAVING A PIE-EATING CONTEST.
PERFECT...

THAT'S JUST THE KIND OF GLUTTONY I'D EXPECT FROM THEM.

YOU WANT TO ENTER IT, DON'T YOU?
I SEE IT MORE AS A CULTURAL EXCHANGE.

SHERMAN'S LAGOON

NEW SHELL?
YEP. HERMIT CRAB MATING SEASON IS UPON US.

MATCHING SHOES.
DAPPER.

AND I DON'T DETECT THAT ROTTEN FISH ODOR THAT USUALLY FOLLOWS YOU AROUND.
I'M TAKING PERSONAL HYGIENE MORE SERIOUSLY.

THE GIANT CLAW SHOULD MAKE THE LADIES' HEADS TURN.
LOOKS REAL, DOESN'T IT?

SO, LEMME GET THIS STRAIGHT. YOU'RE HOPING TO ATTRACT A MATE BY BECOMING SOMETHING YOU'RE NOT.
MORE OR LESS.

WOULDN'T IT BE BETTER TO FIND A FEMALE CRAB THAT FITS THE REAL YOU?

THAT THOUGHT FRIGHTENS ME.
ME TOO, ACTUALLY.

I GOTTA GET INTO THAT PIE-EATING CONTEST.

WE'LL HAVE TO GET KAHUNA TO MAKE US HUMAN.

"US"?
DUH. YOU'LL NEED ME AS YOUR MANAGER.

I'LL HANDLE THE ENTRY FORMS AND STUFF SO YOU CAN FOCUS ON WHAT YOU DO BEST.

DISAPPOINT MY WIFE?
OKAY, SECOND BEST.

OH, GREAT KAHUNA, CAN YOU MAKE US HUMAN? BRIEFLY?
FOR IMPORTANT REASON?

WELL, THERE'S THIS PIE-EATING CONTEST, YOU SEE...
KAHUNA SAY NO!! WASTE OF POWERS FOR SILLY REASON!

WE'LL BRING YOU A T-SHIRT.
XXXXXXXXL.

SO NOW WE'RE HUMANS. WHAT NEXT?
REGISTER FOR THE PIE-EATING CONTEST.

HI, I'M SHERMAN. I NEED TO ENTER THE CONTEST.
WHICH CATEGORY? AMATEUR OR PRO?
Regist.

WELL, UP UNTIL A FEW MINUTES AGO, I WAS A GREAT WHITE SHARK, SO I GUESS I'M A PRO.
SHERMAN!!

YOU SPEED EATERS ARE A WEIRD BREED.
ONE SECOND. MY CRAB NEEDS ME.

OKAY, SHERMAN, LET'S CHECK OUT THE PIE EATING COMPETITION.
COMPETITIO AREA

OOH! ISN'T THAT KIMBO HAKATORI?
I'VE SEEN HIM ON YOUTUBE.

HE WINS ALL THE EATING CONTESTS... HOT DOGS, PIES, WINGS, BURGERS. HE'S A GOD.

HE'S ALSO SINGLE AND BLOGS FROM HIS MOTHER'S BASEMENT.
GO FIGURE.

SHERMAN, THE PIE EATING CONTEST IS IN FIVE MINUTES.
COMPETITION AREA

YOU NEED TO GET MENTALLY PREPARED FOR IT. I WANT YOU TO CLOSE YOUR EYES...
COMPETITION AREA

NOW IMAGINE EATING 20 PIES... ONE PIE... TWO PIES... DOWN THE HATCH... ALL THE WAY TO 20.
COMPETITION

BURP!
YOU'RE READY.
COMPETITIO

YOU DID IT, SHERMAN! YOU WON THE FIRST ROUND OF THE PIE-EATING CONTEST!
AREA

IN THE QUARTER FINALS YOU FACE KIMBO HAKATORI, SO REST UP AND GET PREPARED.
COMPETITION AREA
6

COMPETITION AREA
CRUNCH
CRUNCH
CRUNCH

CHEETO?
AND NO SNACKING BETWEEN PIE-EATING CONTESTS!

SHERMAN'S LAGOON

HEY, PETE, LOOK WHAT JUST SWAM INTO OUR LAGOON. A PUFFERFISH.
REALLY?

YOU'RE NOT ALONE ANYMORE. GO OVER AND SAY "HI" TO HER.

NOW YOU'RE GETTING ALL NERVOUS. DON'T BE NERVOUS.

THE WAY I SEE IT, YOU HAVE TWO OPTIONS. SWIM OVER AND SAY "HI"...

...OR LET HER SWIM AWAY, AND SPEND THE REST OF YOUR LIFE WONDERING WHAT COULD HAVE BEEN.

KABOOM!

I GUESS IF YOU'RE A PUFFERFISH THERE'S A THIRD OPTION.
EXPLODE.

SHERMAN! YOU DID IT! YOU WON THE PIE-EATING CONTEST!
URP!

MISSION ACCOMPLISHED. AND JUST IN THE KNICK OF TIME...
COMPETITION AREA

AT EXACTLY HIGH NOON, WE TRANSFORM FROM HUMANS BACK TO SEA CREATURES...

TRANSITION COMPLETE... ALMOST.
I HAD TIGHTIE WHITIES THAT WHOLE TIME?

AND WHAT'S YOUNG ERNEST UP TO THIS FINE DAY?
WRITING.
TAP
TAP
TAP

ISN'T THAT REFRESHING? A YOUNGSTER USING HIS BRAIN FOR CREATIVE PURPOSES.
TAP
TAP
TAP

THESE DAYS, WE SEE WAY TOO MANY KIDS JUST PLAYING VIDEO GAMES.
TAP
TAP

WHAT ARE YOU WRITING? A SHORT STORY? A POEM? A SONG?
COMPUTER VIRUS.

WELL, I DID IT. I RELEASED MY COMPUTER VIRUS TO THE WORLD.
TAP

MY BEAUTIFUL CREATION HAS BEEN UNLEASHED TO WREAK UNTOLD HAVOC AND DESTRUCTION!
BWA HA HA HA HA HA!
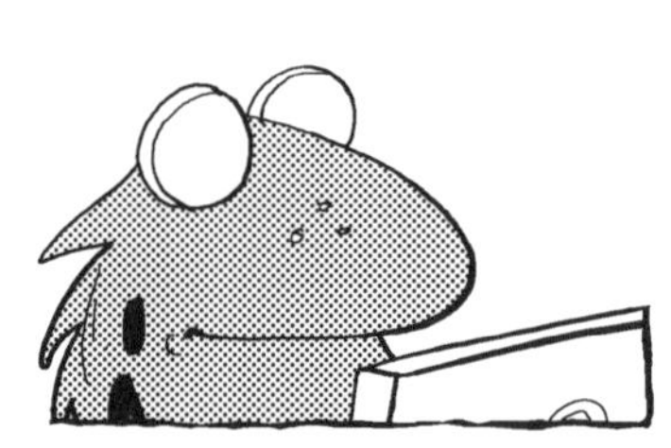

CAN YOU HELP ME OUT WITH THE EVIL GENIUS LAUGH?
IT'S GOTTA COME FROM THE DIAPHRAGM.

THE WORLD IS ON EDGE TONIGHT AS THE "SMELLS FISHY" COMPUTER VIRUS SPREADS.

THERE SEEMS TO BE NO STOPPING IT! IT'S INFECTING EVERYTHING!

MY TELEPROMPTER'S DOWN! RUN FOR YOUR LIVES! THIS IS THE END!

I'VE SEEN DIANE SAWYER MORE PROFESSIONAL.

HER IMPROVISATION NEEDS WORK.

SOMETHING'S WRONG.
WHAT?

I CAN'T GET ON TO FACEBOOK.
ERNEST'S COMPUTER VIRUS HAS GOT TO US!

YOU DIDN'T OPEN ANY EMAILS FROM PEOPLE YOU DON'T KNOW, DID YOU?
ME? NO!

JUST THIS ONE FROM THE FINANCE MINISTER OF NIGERIA, WHO APPARENTLY KNOWS ME FROM SOMEWHERE.
WE'RE SUNK.

FILLMORE, I NEED TO USE YOUR COMPUTER!

CAN'T. THAT COMPUTER VIRUS WIPED ME OUT.
NOOOO!!

THIS IS LIFE OR DEATH STUFF! I'VE GOT TO GET ONLINE!

NEED TO CHECK FACEBOOK?
I'M THIS CLOSE TO CRACKING THE FIVE FRIENDS BARRIER!

SHERMAN'S
LAGOON

FILLMORE, YOU'RE AN EXPERT AT THE SUBTLETIES OF THE ENGLISH LANGUAGE. CAN YOU HELP ME OUT?
I'LL TRY.

I GOT AN EMAIL FROM THIS GIRL I REALLY LIKE. I WANT YOU TO READ IT.

"DEAR HAWTHORNE..."
IF SHE LIKED ME, WOULD SHE OPEN UP WITH THAT?

WOULDN'T SHE JUST SAY "HI"? OR "HEY"?
SEEMS A BIT FORMAL.

"HOW R U?"
SHE CARES ABOUT ME.
NO. SHE'S JUST SAYING THAT.

"SORRY I TOOK SO LONG TO ANSWER YOUR EMAIL."
SHE'S REVEALING DEEP SECRETS TO ME ABOUT HER FEELINGS.
NO. SHE'S JUST SAYING THAT.

"I AM GOOD."
"I AM GOOD" AS IN, "IF YOU WANT TO ASK ME OUT, I AM GOOD WITH THAT"?
NO. SHE'S JUST SAYING THAT.

"I HOPE I NEVER SEE YOU AGAIN."
SHE'S JUST SAYING THAT.

HAWTHORNE! WHAT ARE YOU DOING ABOUT THE CRISIS?!
HUH?
MAYOR'S OFFICE

AS MAYOR OF THIS LAGOON, IT'S UP TO YOU TO TAKE CONTROL!
HOW?

WE NEED TO STOP THIS COMPUTER VIRUS! DO SOMETHING! CALL OUT THE NATIONAL GUARD!

I'M THE NATIONAL GUARD?
IT'S A ROTATING THING. I WAS GOING TO SEND AN EMAIL.

WHAT'S THAT?
A LETTER.

WITH ALL THE COMPUTERS DOWN, THERE'S NO EMAIL.

RIGHT.

BUT YOU CAN STILL COMMUNICATE WITH THESE "LETTERS"?
YES. IT WILL GET HAND DELIVERED.

ARE THERE ELVES INVOLVED?
IF IT HELPS YOU UNDERSTAND.

HOW ARE YOU ENJOYING LIFE WITHOUT THE INTERNET?
IT'S RATHER NICE.

IT'S A CHANCE TO CONVERSE WITH REAL FRIENDS, NOT JUST FACEBOOK FRIENDS.

WITH REAL FRIENDS, I FIND I'M RARELY "ROLLING ON THE FLOOR LAUGHING."
AND THEN THERE'S THE BAD BREATH.

WHAT ARE YOU DOING?
READING A NEWSPAPER.

NOW THAT ERNEST'S COMPUTER VIRUS HAS BROUGHT THE ENTIRE INTERNET DOWN, I'M GETTING NEWS THE OLD-FASHIONED WAY.

FUNNY THING ABOUT READING THE NEWS IN A NEWSPAPER...

EVERYONE KNOWS YOU'RE NOT WORKING.
THAT'S WHY I'M HIDING IT BEHIND MY COMPUTER.

ERNEST, YOU'RE BACK AT YOUR COMPUTER.
YEP. I'M ELIMINATING THE VIRUS I CREATED.

SOON, WE'LL ALL BE ABLE TO USE THE INTERNET AGAIN.

BEING WITHOUT THE NET HAS MADE ME REALIZE HOW UTTERLY DEPENDENT ON TECHNOLOGY WE'VE ALL BECOME.

THERE'S A FERRET TICKLING A CAT ON YOUTUBE.
YES! CIVILIZATION IS BACK, BABY!

WELL, I'M HEADING OFF THROUGH THE PIPES.
BON VOYAGE.

WHO KNOWS WHERE IT WILL LEAD ME. BUT WE KNOW IT WILL INVOLVE FUN AND ADVENTURE.

IS THIS THE LINE FOR FUN AND ADVENTURE?
STARBUCKS.

SHERMAN'S LAGOON

"A DAY IN THE LIFE OF A SEA TURTLE," TAKE ONE. ACTION!

CAN'T YOU DO SOMETHING A LITTLE MORE EXCITING?
THIS IS WHAT SEA TURTLES DO.

CUT.
OKAY. WAIT HERE.

HEY! I THOUGHT THIS WAS A SEA TURTLE DOCUMENTARY!
WE NEED A SHARK TO GIVE IT SOME SIZZLE.

THAT'S IT. THAT'S OUR CONFLICT...
TAKE TWO... ACTION!

THE RUTHLESS SAVAGE OF THE SEA SWIMS INTO VIEW.... THE OTHER ANIMALS TREMBLE AT HIS APPROACH.

STOP PICKING YOUR NOSE!

WHERE'S HAWTHORNE?
GONE.

BUT HE WAS SO YOUNG.
WELL... YOUNGISH.
HE JUST WENT THROUGH THE PIPES.

OOH! NO DOUBT TO SOME EXOTIC, MAGICAL PLACE.

QUIT SNIFFING ME LIKE THAT!
HE HAS A GREETING DISORDER.

WHERE AM I, ANYWAY?
THIS IS THE DOG POUND.

WHERE CUTE DOGS GET ADOPTED, AND UGLY ONES NEVER GET OUT.

HOW ARE YOU AT LOOKING CUTE? SHOW ME YOUR CUTE FACE.
HMMM...

HOW ARE YOU AT DIGGING TUNNELS? SHOW ME YOUR TUNNEL-DIGGING FACE.

BOY, LIFE IN THIS DOG MUST BE TOUGH, HUH?

ONCE YOU FIND THE RIGHT PACK TO HANG WITH, IT'S NOT SO BAD.

WHICH PACK SHOULD I JOIN? THE PIT BULLS? THE DOBERMANS?
I'VE GOT JUST THE PACK FOR YOU.

HOW DO THOSE EYEBALLS PHYSICALLY STAY IN YOUR SKULL?
I DON'T LIKE THIS GRINGO.

HAWTHORNE, YOU STILL HAVEN'T TOLD ME WHAT BREED OF DOG YOU ARE.

I'M A VIZSLA.
I'M A...
UH...

POLYNESIAN STUD MUFFIN.

YOU LOOK LIKE A HERMIT CRAB.
I DIDN'T SAY I WAS A PUREBREED.

HI, I'M HAWTHORNE.
MY NAME'S POOKIE.

I'M HEAD OF THE SOCIAL COMMITTEE IN THIS DOG POUND.

NOTHING HAPPENS IN THIS JOINT WITHOUT MY APPROVAL. QUESTIONS?

CAN YOU TEACH ME THE BUTT SCOOT? IT'S HARDER THAN IT LOOKS.
GUARDS!

LEMME SHOW YOU AROUND THE POUND, HAWTHORNE.

OVER HERE IS THE DINING AREA... RESTROOMS ARE DOWN THE HALL...

OVER THERE'S THE DOG LOUNGE.

AND HERE'S OUR SCRATCH 'N SNIFF LIBRARY.
WOW. I WANNA BE A DOG.

SHERMAN'S Lagoon
SHARK LOANS

HELLO. I'D LIKE TO BORROW SOME MONEY.
OKAY. HOW MUCH?
SHARK LOANS

A HUNDRED DOLLARS.
HERE YOU GO.

THANKS. BYE.
SHARK LOANS

YOU'RE NOT A VERY GOOD LOAN SHARK.
HUH?

LOAN SHARKS ARE INTIMIDATING AND RUTHLESS. LEMME SEE RUTHLESS.
GRRR.

HELLO. I'D LIKE TO BORROW SOME MONEY.
GOOD HEAVENS. YOU APPEAR TO BE MORTALLY WOUNDED AND BLEEDING PROFUSELY.

THAT'S JUST... UH... KETCHUP.
OKAY. HERE'S A HUNDRED DOLLARS.
THANKS. BYE.

YOU'RE NOT EVEN A VERY GOOD SHARK, ARE YOU?
HUH?

WHO ARE YOU ALL WAITING FOR?
THE MOST EVIL THING ON THE PLANET. THE MAILMAN.

HE COMES AROUND THIS TIME OF DAY AND TRIES TO LEAVE MAIL. ALL DOGS HAVE SWORN AN OATH TO PREVENT THIS FROM HAPPENING.

EXCEPT NOWADAYS, MOST MAIL IS DELIVERED THROUGH THE INTERNET.

IT WAS INVENTED TO GET AROUND DOGS, YOU KNOW.
I DID NOT KNOW THAT.

YOU'RE LEAVING US?
YES, I'M HEADING HOME.

WHY?
I'M JUST NOT CUT OUT FOR THE DOG'S LIFE.

I'M A CRAB. I LIVE IN THE OCEAN. I NEED WATER. COOL, CLEAR, FRESH WATER.

TOILET WATER'S NOT GOOD ENOUGH FOR YOU, HUH?
NO.
GOTTA GO.

LOOK. QUIGLEY'S TRYING TO CATCH ME AGAIN.
AND SOONER OR LATER, HE'S GOING TO GET YOU.

YOU NEED TO SNEAK UP ON HIM. TRY AND FIGURE OUT WHAT HIS STRATEGY FOR KILLING YOU IS.
GOT IT.

I'LL LURE HIM IN WITH THIS BOX OF DING DONGS.
DING DONGS

I'M DEFENSELESS.
THEN DIBS ON YOUR WII.

DANG! ANOTHER CLOSE ONE!

I CAN'T GO ON LIKE THIS. QUIGLEY'S GONNA KILL ME!
YOU KNOW WHAT YOU NEED TO DO?

MAKE QUIGLEY YOUR "FRENEMY." YOU BOTH NEED EACH OTHER. MAKE HIM UNDERSTAND THAT.

LET'S SEE... EVENTS... MESSAGES... LIKE... COMMENT... FRIENDS... I'M NOT SEEING HOW TO "FRENEMY" SOMEONE.
NOT EVERYTHING IS SOLVED WITH FACEBOOK.

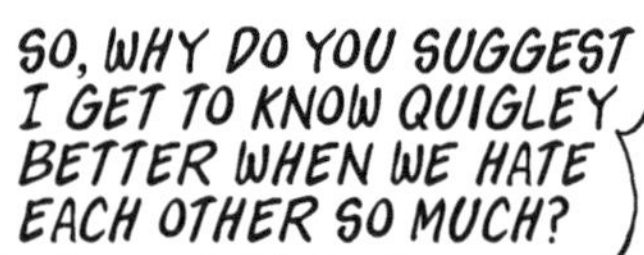
SO, WHY DO YOU SUGGEST I GET TO KNOW QUIGLEY BETTER WHEN WE HATE EACH OTHER SO MUCH?

HAVE YOU HEARD THE PHRASE "KEEP YOUR FRIENDS CLOSE, AND YOUR ENEMIES CLOSER"?

NO.
OKAY...

HOW ABOUT THE PHRASE "YOU'RE A BIG DUMB SHARK"?
THAT ONE'S POPULAR AT FAMILY GATHERINGS.

KAHUNA TURN YOU INTO HUMAN, SO YOU CAN MAKE FRENEMIES WITH QUIGLEY.
THANKS!

AND FILLMORE, TOO!
HUH?!

POOF!
POOF!

WHY'D YOU DRAG ME INTO THIS?
BOY, THAT JELLYFISH BREATH IS NOT ATTRACTIVE ON A HUMAN.

SHERMAN'S LAGOON

LOVELY DAY.
NO, IT'S NOT.

HOW COME YOU'RE HAPPY ALL THE TIME?

IT'S JUST A MATTER OF HOW YOU APPROACH LIFE.

ENJOY THE HAPPY MOMENTS WHEN THEY COME...

AND DELETE THE BAD MOMENTS FROM YOUR MEMORY.
HMPH!

DELETE THEM AS SOON AS THEY'RE OVER, AND YOU'LL BE LOOKING BACK ON A HAPPY LIFE.

I'VE ALREADY DELETED THIS CONVERSATION.
HMPH!

OKAY, WE'RE HUMANS NOW, SHERMAN. LET'S FIND QUIGLEY AND HIRE HIM AS A FISHING GUIDE.
RIGHT.
Charter Boat for Hire

THAT WAY I CAN REALLY GET TO KNOW MY ENEMY.
EXACTLY.

REMEMBER. WE'RE JUST A COUPLE OF DUDES AND WE WANT TO GO FISHING. GOT IT?
GOT IT.

HELLO. CAN YOU HELP US YANK INNOCENT FISH FROM THEIR FAMILIES?
SMOOTH.

REMEMBER, ASK QUIGLEY ABOUT HIS NEMESIS, THE SHARK.
Charter

HE HATES ANOTHER SHARK BESIDES ME?
NO, I MEANT YOU. BUT, YOU'RE A HUMAN AT THE MOMENT.

OH, RIGHT.
KINDA CONFUSING, ISN'T IT?

SO, YOU GONNA SPEAR ME AT SOME POINT?
ONLY IF YOU DON'T PAY ME.

IT WAS 20 YEARS AGO THAT SHARK TOOK MY LEG OFF.
AND YOU STILL HOLD A GRUDGE?

I'LL GO TO MY GRAVE HATING THAT FOUL BEAST WITH EVERY FIBER OF MY BEING.

WHAT IF I TOLD YOU I AM THAT SHARK? I'VE CHANGED INTO A HUMAN TO HELP YOU GET CLOSURE.

HUG?
WHAT HAVE YOU HEARD ABOUT MY CHARTERS?

YOU'RE BACK.
WE HAD TO LEAVE IN A HURRY. I THOUGHT QUIGLEY WAS GOING TO KILL US.

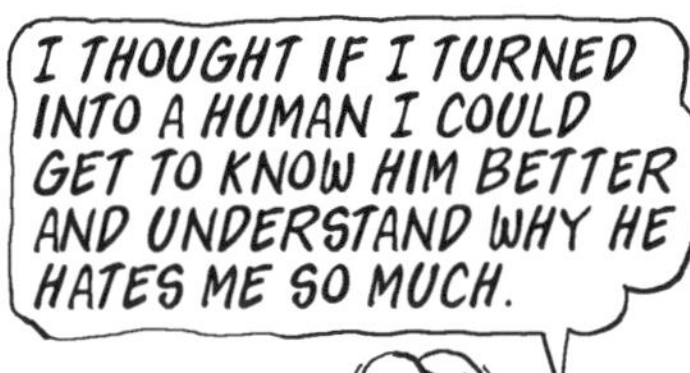
I THOUGHT IF I TURNED INTO A HUMAN I COULD GET TO KNOW HIM BETTER AND UNDERSTAND WHY HE HATES ME SO MUCH.

SOME THINGS DEFY UNDERSTANDING... LIKE WHY SOME PEOPLE HATE ME SO MUCH.

I CAN UNDERSTAND WHY SOME PEOPLE HATE YOU SO MUCH.
PRAY, TELL.

WHAT'S THAT?
A FLIER I FOUND UP ON THE BEACH.

ANOTHER LOST DOG?
NOPE. IT'S A PHOTOGRAPHY CONTEST.

OUTDOOR PHOTOGRAPHY?
UNDERWATER.
PROFESSIONAL?
AMATEUR.
COLOR?
BLACK AND WHITE.

DO YOU WANT TO JUST **READ** IT?
NOT THAT INTERESTED.

THERE'S A PHOTOGRAPHY CONTEST?
YEP. THE BEACH APES ARE HAVING ONE.

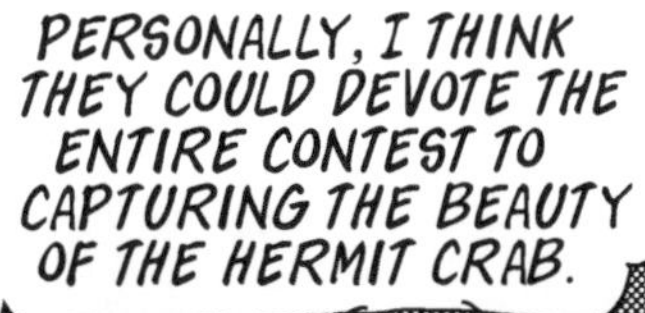
PERSONALLY, I THINK THEY COULD DEVOTE THE ENTIRE CONTEST TO CAPTURING THE BEAUTY OF THE HERMIT CRAB.

DO YOU EVEN **OWN** A MIRROR?
WE'VE GOT INNER BEAUTY, JERKFACE!

SHERMAN'S LAGOON

WHAT A GORGEOUS DAY!
PERFECT DAY FOR GARDENING...

AND FOR BUILDING THAT FLOWER BOX YOU KEEP PROMISING ME YOU'RE GOING TO BUILD.

IT'S ON MY LIST.
WHERE'S YOUR LIST?

I'VE GOT IT WRITTEN RIGHT HERE ON MY FIN.

DO YOU HAVE "FIX LEAKY TOILET" WRITTEN ON YOUR FIN?

UMM...
NO.
HERE, ALLOW ME.

I'LL ADD A FEW MORE THINGS WHILE I'M AT IT.

AMAZING... AND YOU STILL HAVE FOUR HOURS TO PLAY GOLF.
IT'S ALL ABOUT TIME MANAGEMENT.

SPORTING A NEW SHELL TODAY, HUH?
THIS OLD THING?

WOULDN'T HAVE ANYTHING TO DO WITH THE UNDERWATER PHOTOGRAPHY CONTEST THAT'S GOING ON, WOULD IT?
NO!

I COULDN'T CARE LESS ABOUT THAT.
SURE.

YOU SURE THAT'S NOT A GIRL'S SHELL?
UNISEX! BIG DIFFERENCE!

THE UNDERWATER PHOTOGRAPHERS ARE HERE TO TAKE PICTURES OF US.
WHATEVER.

I'M GONNA TRY SOME OF MY BODY-BUILDING POSES.
SHERMAN...

THEY JUST WANT US TO BE NATURAL. THAT'S WHAT MAKES GOOD PHOTOGRAPHY.

ARE THOSE WHITENING STRIPS ON YOUR TEETH?
IT WAS A MAINTENANCE DAY! PURE COINCIDENCE!

HEY, ERNEST, YOU HEARD ABOUT THE UNDERWATER PHOTOGRAPHY CONTEST THAT'S GOING ON?

YEAH.

THE WINNING PHOTO GETS INTO NATIONAL GEOGRAPHIC.
I KNOW.

DO YOU THINK THEY'LL GO FOR SOMETHING IN THE HUMOROUS VEIN?
WHAT ARE YOU GONNA DO THAT'S FUNNY?

HAVE YOU READ THE TEE SHIRT?
TOO MUCH EFFORT.
I'M WITH STUPID

THERE'S AN UNDERWATER PHOTOGRAPHER!
HOW DO I LOOK?

UMMM... ACTUALLY, THEY'RE SHOOTING FILLMORE.
IS HE...

VOGUING?
LOOKS THAT WAY...

UH OH. HE'S CRAMPING UP.
YOU'RE OLD! STRETCH FIRST!

HERE'S THE NEW NATIONAL GEOGRAPHIC!
OOH! LET'S SEE!

WHICH ONE OF US HAS HIS PICTURE IN IT?
I'M LOOKING! SETTLE DOWN!
NATIONAL GEOGRAPHIC

HUH?!
THORNTON?!

DID YOU KNOW YOU'RE THE NEW FACE OF CLIMATE CHANGE?
TALK TO MY AGENT.

HEY, FAT BOY, HAVE YOU EVER CONSIDERED CHANGING DOCTORS?

I GUESS.
BUT WHO?

TA-DAH!
IS THAT A MAIL-ORDER MEDICAL DIPLOMA?
DIPLOMA OF MEDICINE

FROM THE SAME FOLKS WHO MADE ME A PRIEST AND AN ASTRONAUT.
YOU'RE GETTING QUITE A RESUME.

SHERMAN'S
LAGOON

WHAT'S THIS?
A POWER OF ATTORNEY.

I WANT YOU TO HANDLE ALL OF MY AFFAIRS WHILE I'M GONE.

WHERE ARE YOU GOING?
I'M HAVING MYSELF CRYOGENICALLY FROZEN.

I'VE LEFT INSTRUCTIONS TO THAW ME OUT WHEN THINGS GET BETTER.

WHAT THINGS?
JUST THINGS IN GENERAL.

WHAT IF IT DOESN'T GET BETTER? WHAT IF IT GETS WORSE?
LEAVE ME FROZEN.

LOOK. IT'S REAL SIMPLE. IF THINGS ARE BETTER, THAW ME. IF THEY'RE NOT, DON'T. GOT IT?

WHAT IF IT'S BETTER BECAUSE YOU'RE FROZEN?
THAT'S A DILEMMA.

OH, NO. SAY IT AIN'T SO, HAWTHORNE.
THAT'S **DOCTOR** HAWTHORNE.
Doc in a Box

DID I SOMEHOW NOT NOTICE THE TWELVE YEARS YOU WERE AWAY AT MEDICAL SCHOOL?

I GOT A MAIL-IN DEGREE IN MEDICINE. IT'S ALL LEGIT.

LOOK. IT'S SIGNED BY SOME BIG-TIME PHYSICIAN.
DR. SEUSS.

I'D LIKE TO SEE THE DOCTOR.
STEP INTO THE EXAM ROOM.
Doc in a Box

WHAT'S TROUBLING YOU?
FEELING A LITTLE NAUSEOUS LATELY.
BE RIGHT BACK.

QUICK SEARCH ON GOOGLE FOR "NAUSEOUS."
HMMMM...
TAP TAP TAP

TURNS OUT YOU'RE PREGNANT.
MEGAN'S NOT GOING TO LIKE THIS ONE BIT.

DR. HAWTHORNE, I DON'T THINK I'M PREGNANT.
THE SIGNS ARE THERE.

NAUSEA, HUGE GUT, YOU EAT LIKE A PIG.
BUT I'M NOT A FEMALE SHARK.

AND I'M PRETTY SURE THEY'RE THE ONES WHO HAVE THE BABIES.
LEMME CHECK SOMETHING.

HOW ARE THE OVARIES?
SQUISHY... WAIT. THAT'S A BOOGER.

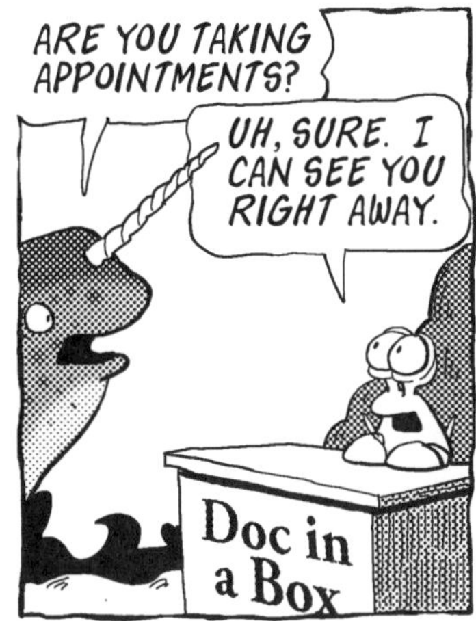
ARE YOU TAKING APPOINTMENTS?
UH, SURE. I CAN SEE YOU RIGHT AWAY.
Doc in a Box

WHAT SEEMS TO BE THE TROUBLE?
STOMACH PAIN.
BE RIGHT BACK.

OKAY, GOOGLE, HELP ME OUT. LARGE SMELLY ANIMAL WITH TWISTY HORN... STOMACH PAIN...
HMMMM...

GOOD NEWS! UNICORNS DON'T ACTUALLY EXIST. YOU'LL BE FINE.
I'M A NARWHAL.

DON'T WORRY, THIS OPEN-HEART SURGERY WILL MAKE YOU FEEL LIKE A NEW OCTOPUS.
YOU'RE THE DOCTOR.

HOLY CEPHALOPOD! YOU HAVE THREE HEARTS!

ALL OCTOPUSES HAVE THREE HEARTS... DOCTOR.

COOL. GUESS WHOSE BILL JUST TRIPLED?
UMH.

HEY, DOC, ARE YOU SEEING PATIENTS TODAY?
SORRY, SHERMAN.
Doc in a Box

I'VE HAD TO TURN IN MY MAIL-ORDER MEDICAL DEGREE. THE LAWSUITS ARE PILING UP.
WHOA!

ALL THIS HAS HELPED ME DECIDE WHERE I WANT TO DO NEXT WITH MY LIFE.

MAIL-ORDER LAW DEGREE?
CALL ME COUNSELOR.
Doc in a Box

Sherman's Lagoon

'SUP?
ERNEST, YOU'RE JUST THE GUY I WAS LOOKING FOR.

I GOT MYSELF ONE OF THESE NEW-FANGLED PHONES...

I WANT TO ADD BOB THE BOTTOM DWELLER, HERE, TO MY LIST OF CONTACTS.

CLICK ON "CONTACTS," THEN "ADD," THEN HIT THE RETURN BUTTON.

NOW TYPE IN "BOB THE BOTTOM DWELLER."
THAT WAS EASY.

OKAY, NOW DELETE CARL.
LET'S SEE IF I CAN DO THIS...

SWARMS OF JELLYFISH HAVE BEEN SEEN ALL OVER THE WORLD.
Lagoon Tribune
JELLYFISH INVASION

AND IN SOME PLACES WHERE JELLYFISH DON'T NORMALLY GO.
Lagoon Tribune
JELLYFISH INVASION

LIKE WALMART?
NO, I THINK THEY'VE ALWAYS BEEN BARGAIN SHOPPERS.

LOOKS LIKE THE JELLYFISH EXPLOSION HAS COME TO OUR LAGOON. BE CAREFUL.

NOT TO WORRY. SHARKS HAVE A THICK, PROTECTIVE SKIN THAT'S PRETTY MUCH IMMUNE TO JELLYFISH STINGS.

OWWWWOOOO!

NOT EVERYTHING YOU READ ABOUT SHARKS IS TRUE.
CURSE YOU, WIKIPEDIA!

SURE ARE A LOT OF JELLYFISH AROUND HERE.
YUP. SHERMAN ALREADY GOT STUNG.

WEIRD THING IS, HE SEEMS DIFFERENT NOW, AFTER BEING STUNG... SMARTER.
NO WAY.

HEY FAT BOY, WHAT'S THE SQUARE ROOT OF SIXTEEN?
FOUR.

SEE? SAME STUPID SHERMAN.
ACTUALLY...

WEIRD HOW BEING STUNG BY A JELLYFISH MADE SHERMAN SMARTER.
HE COULDN'T GET ANY MORE STUPID.

I'M SURE SOME SILLY JELLYFISH STING WOULDN'T CHANGE ME IN THE LEAST.

OWWW!

HOW DO YOU FEEL?
LIKE GIVING TO A CHARITY... WHATEVER THAT IS.

HAWTHORNE, I DETECT A CHANGE IN YOUR PERSONALITY, TOO, AFTER BEING STUNG BY THAT JELLYFISH.

YEAH. WEIRD. I'M SUDDENLY FEELING ALL GENEROUS AND TOLERANT. I DON'T KNOW WHAT'S GOTTEN INTO ME.

WOW. SHERMAN GETS STUNG, AND HE BECOMES SMART... NOW YOU BECOME... DECENT.

PERHAPS A STING IS IN ORDER FOR YOU.
I'M THE NORMAL ONE AROUND HERE!!

IT'S JUST PLAIN WEIRD AROUND HERE EVER SINCE EVERYONE UNDERWENT THOSE PERSONALITY CHANGES...

ESPECIALLY HAWTHORNE. I JUST CAN'T GET USED TO HIM BEING SO CHARITABLE.

I'M RAISING FUNDS TO HELP THE BLIND. ANYBODY IN?

FIRST, OF COURSE, WE'LL NEED TO BLIND SOME FOLKS.
HE'S STILL GETTING THE HANG OF IT.

SHERMAN'S LAGOON

BEHOLD, THE CHUBBY PINK TOES OF A HAIRLESS BEACH APE.

WHICH ONE OF YOU WOULD LIKE TO BE PINCHED FIRST? COME TO PAPA.

SOMETHING WRONG?
I'M NOT FEELING IT TODAY.

I DON'T HAVE THE REQUIRED ANGER TO DO THIS PROPERLY.
I CAN HELP.

CLOSE YOUR EYES. NOW, THINK OF SOMETHING FROM YOUR PAST THAT STILL MAKES YOU MAD.

AAUUGH!!

WHAT WAS THAT FOR?!
YOUR LOUSY BIRTHDAY PRESENT!
THERAPY BACKFIRE.

I WONDER WHY THE JELLYFISH HAVEN'T BOTHERED YOU.
THE BOND.

SEA TURTLES AND JELLYFISH HAVE A CERTAIN... SHALL WE SAY... SYMPATICO.
I SEE...
OPERA NEWS

OW!!
BOND BROKEN.
OPERA NEWS

NOW WE MUST OBSERVE **YOU** FOR PERSONALITY CHANGES.
I'M HANKERING FOR A BEER AND A TRACTOR PULL.
OPERA NEWS

I'VE GOT AN URGE TO CHEW ON A LICENSE PLATE... PREFERABLY SOMETHING SOUTHWEST.
WHAT ARE YOU? STUPID?

I THINK MY PERSONALITY CHANGE HAS WORN OFF. I DON'T FEEL SMART ANYMORE.
AND I'M NOT FEELING SO KIND ANYMORE.

I WONDER IF FILLMORE'S BACK TO HIS NORMAL POMPOUS SELF.
LET'S GO SEE.

CHECK OUT MY GUNS. I NAMED 'EM LYNYRD AND SKYNYRD.
I ACTUALLY PREFER THIS VERSION.

I THINK MEGAN WANTS TO VISIT THE BAHAMAS.

BECAUSE OF THE NEW SHARK SANCTUARY THERE?
HOW DID YOU KNOW ABOUT IT?

BECAUSE I **READ**.
HEY! I READ PLENTY!

NOT A LOT OF NEWS IN COMIC BOOKS.
THEY'RE CALLED "GRAPHIC NOVELS."

AUGH! HUMANS!
RELAX, SHERMAN.
Welcome to the BAHAMAS

THAT'S ALL PART OF THE ECO-TOURISM EXPERIENCE HERE IN THE BAHAMAS.

HAIRLESS BEACH APES ACTUALLY ENJOY SWIMMING WITH SHARKS, APPARENTLY.
INTERESTING.

CAN I SET OUT A TIP JAR?
THE CLASSIER SHARKS DO.

THIS SHARK SANCTUARY IS HARD TO GET USED TO.
BUT THE BAHAMAS ARE LOVELY.

BUT I'VE BEEN CONDITIONED TO FEAR HUMANS, NOT SWIM WITH THEM.

OUR SPECIES DON'T MIX. WE HAVE ABSOLUTELY ZERO COMMONALITY.

SAID THE GUY WHO ORDERED THE MINI CORN DOGS WITH CHEESE IN THE MIDDLE.
THEY DID GET THOSE RIGHT.

WHERE'S SHERMAN BEEN?
BAHAMAS. THERE'S A NEW SHARK SANCTUARY.

TRYING TO BREAK THROUGH GENERATIONS OF FEAR, MISTRUST AND DISRESPECT BETWEEN SHARKS AND HUMANS.

YOU SURE HE'S NOT AT FAT CAMP?
NOT 100 PERCENT.

SHERMAN'S
LAGOON

I SEEM TO HAVE DEVELOPED A LITTLE RED BUMP ON MY SNOUT.

WHAT DO YOU THINK IT IS?
LET'S SEE WHAT THE INTERNET SAYS ABOUT IT.

"RED" "BUMP" "SNOUT"
WHAT IS IT?
HMMM...
TAP TAP TAP TAP

YOU'RE NOT FEELING ITCHY ALL OVER, ARE YOU?
WELL, NOW THAT YOU MENTION IT, I DO FEEL KIND OF ITCHY ALL OF A SUDDEN.

FATIGUED?
SINCE THIS RED BUMP HAS COME INTO MY LIFE, I'VE HAD NO ENERGY.

FORGETFULNESS?
I FORGOT TO BRUSH MY TEETH LAST NIGHT!

SORE KNEES?
YES!

YOU DON'T HAVE KNEES.
MY KNEES ARE GONE!!

THERE'S A HUMAN. SWIM ON OVER AND LET HIM TAKE A PHOTO OF YOU.

SEE? THEY DON'T MIND SHARING THE WATER WITH SHARKS. HERE IN THE BAHAMAS, YOU'RE A TOURIST ATTRACTION.

THEY DON'T CARE IF WE PEE IN THE WATER?
SO DO THEY.

TIME TO GO HOME, SHERMAN. OUR BAHAMAS VACATION IS OVER WITH.
WHY CAN'T WE LIVE HERE? I LOVE THIS PLACE.

HERE, THEY REALIZE SHARKS ARE MORE VALUABLE ALIVE THAN DEAD.

WE KEEP THE OCEAN HEALTHY, WE'RE GOOD FOR TOURISM.

YOU CAN BE AN ECONOMIC STIMULUS WITHOUT GETTING OUT OF YOUR CHAIR.
AND THE DAIQUIRIS ARE AWESOME.

HEY, YOU'RE BACK. HOW WAS THE BAHAMAS SHARK SANCTUARY?
TERRIFIC!

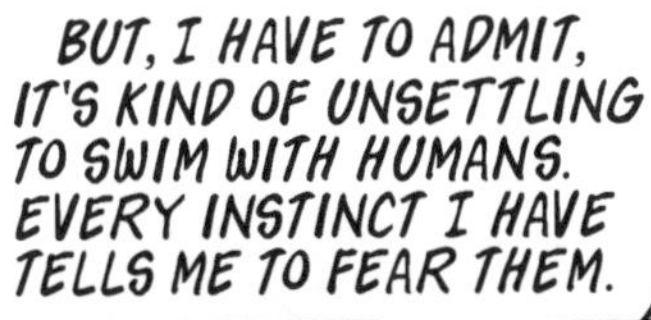
BUT, I HAVE TO ADMIT, IT'S KIND OF UNSETTLING TO SWIM WITH HUMANS. EVERY INSTINCT I HAVE TELLS ME TO FEAR THEM.

THUNK!

BALANCE RESTORED?
OOH! QUIGLEY'S GONE GRAPHITE.

OH, MARTHA.

DID YOU SAY SOMETHING, SHERMAN?
MARTHA, I MISSED YOU, TOO.

MARTHA?!
NO KISSING YET, MY DEAR.

MY WOODEN TEETH NEED A GOOD BRUSHING.
HE'S CHEATING ON ME HUNDREDS OF YEARS AGO.

WERE YOU HAVING WEIRD DREAMS LAST NIGHT?
DON'T THINK SO. WHY?

YOU WERE SPEAKING JIBBERISH... STUFF ABOUT MARTHA AND WOODEN TEETH.

ALMOST LIKE YOU WERE DREAMING YOU WERE THE FIRST PRESIDENT.

HARVEY FINKLESTEIN?
NOT OF OUR ROTARY CLUB.

SOMETHING ODD HAS BEEN GOING ON WITH SHERMAN.
HAS HE BEEN BRUSHING HIS TEETH?

HE'S HAVING RECURRING DREAMS ABOUT BEING GEORGE WASHINGTON... TALKING IN HIS SLEEP... SAYING STRANGE THINGS.
HMMM...

PERHAPS SHERMAN **WAS** GEORGE WASHINGTON IN A PAST LIFE. I'D LIKE TO STUDY THIS.

COULDN'T YOU JUST SIT BY THE BED?
AND FOR CRYING OUT LOUD, PUT YOUR SHELL BACK ON.

SHERMAN'S LAGOON
Background Image by NASA

GOING SOMEWHERE?

THE CRAB NEBULA.
IT'S PRETTY FAR. BETTER PACK A LUNCH.

YOU DOUBT MY RESOLVE?

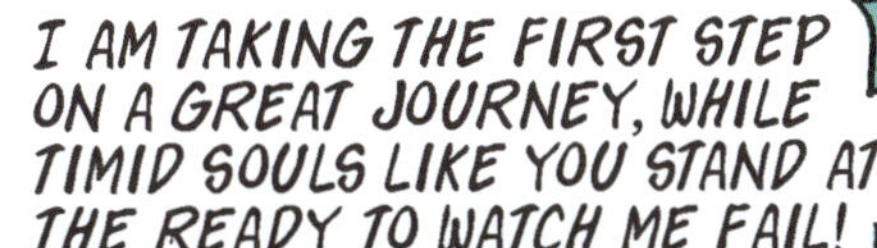
I AM TAKING THE FIRST STEP ON A GREAT JOURNEY, WHILE TIMID SOULS LIKE YOU STAND AT THE READY TO WATCH ME FAIL!

TIMID SOULS LIKE YOU STAND AT THE READY TO SAY, "THAT WAS PRETTY DUMB."

IF YOU CAN DREAM IT, YOU CAN DO IT! PROVIDENCE SMILES ON THE BOLD!

FWOOSH!

AAAAUUGH!
SPLASH!
THAT WAS PRETTY DUMB.

FILLMORE, HE'S TALKING IN HIS SLEEP AGAIN.

FASCINATING.
(SNORT) I WILL CALL THIS NEW MATH "CALCULUS."

I BELIEVE HIS SOUL WAS ONCE IN SIR ISAAC NEWTON.

OW! CURSED APPLE! HIT ME ON THE HEAD! ZZZZZZZ...

AMAZING! WE GET TO HEAR NEWTON'S ACTUAL WORDS THE MOMENT HE DEVISES THE THEORY OF GRAVITY!
SNORT!
ZZZZZZ

NEW THEORY: FRUIT WILL ATTACK EVEN WHEN NOT PROVOKED.
NEVER HEARD THAT PART BEFORE.

HAWTHORNE, WHAT ARE YOU DOING HERE? I'M TRYING TO SLEEP!
WATCHING.

I HEAR YOU'VE BEEN TALKING IN YOUR SLEEP... ABOUT YOUR PAST LIVES. DUDE, THAT'S WEIRD STUFF.

I'M HERE FOR THE SHOW. GO ON - GET STARTED.
KIND OF CREEPY WITH YOU JUST STARING AT ME LIKE THAT.

AND EATING POPCORN.
OH YEAH. GOTTA SILENCE MY CELL PHONE.

HE'S ASLEEP AGAIN.
LET'S SEE IF BECOMES POSSESSED BY ONE OF HIS PAST LIVES.

CHANGE THE ELECTRICAL RESISTANCE AND DO THE EXPERIMENT OVER...
HE'S AN INVENTOR OF SOME KIND.

WATSON! COME QUICK! I NEED YOU!
HE'S ALEXANDER GRAHAM BELL!

WATSON, PLEASE EXPLAIN MY TEXTING PLAN AGAIN.
A LITTLE DUBIOUS.
NO. THOSE THINGS CAN BE TRICKY.

WE WANT TO FURTHER OBSERVE SHERMAN WHILE HE'S SLEEPING.
WHAT'S THE BIG DEAL ABOUT HIS SILLY DREAMS?

MEGAN, WE'RE SEEING EVIDENCE THAT SHERMAN'S SOUL HAS PASSED THROUGH SOME GREAT FIGURES IN HISTORY.
ZZZZZZ

OW! HEY, THAT HURT! QUIT SMACKING ME IN THE BUTT!

NOT SURE ABOUT THIS ONE.
OKAY! GET OFF MY BACK! I'M GOING!
SECRETARIAT.

ARE SHERMAN'S PAST LIVES STILL COMING OUT IN HIS SLEEP?
YEAH. I GUESS SO.
ZZZZZ

BUT I'M STARTING TO SUSPECT THAT SHERMAN MIGHT BE MAKING IT ALL UP.

SOME OF HIS PAST LIVES AREN'T EVEN REAL PEOPLE.

I'LL GET YOU, YOU WASCALLY WABBIT!
WHOA! THE FUDD MAN!
I'M OUT.

WHAT ARE YOU AND YOUR COMPUTER UP TO TODAY, ERNEST?
WRITING SOFTWARE.

WITH THIS SOFTWARE, YOUR IPHONE WILL BE ABLE TO MAKE ALL OF YOUR IMPORTANT LIFE DECISIONS FOR YOU.

NO MORE WORRIES. JUST SET IT AND FORGET IT.

YOU'RE USING YOUR POWERS FOR GOOD?
I'M HAVING AN OFF DAY.

SHERMAN'S LAGOON

WHAT'S THE MATTER, ERNEST?
SOME DAYS I FEEL SO INSIGNIFICANT. LIKE NOBODY KNOWS I'M EVEN HERE.

I REMEMBER WHEN I WAS A KID I USED TO FEEL THAT WAY SOMETIMES.

JUST REMEMBER YOU'RE UNIQUE. YOU'RE ONE OF A KIND.

LOOK! OUT THERE! THAT'S A WORLD WAITING FOR UNIQUE YOU.

THAT WORLD OUT THERE WILL ONE DAY RECOGNIZE THAT **YOU** ARE SOMEBODY SPECIAL.

DON'T LOOK THAT WAY, LOOK THIS WAY.

SHERMAN, MY NEW SOFTWARE IS FINISHED.
COOL!

I NEED YOUR IPHONE TO TEST IT OUT.
UHHH, OKAY.

JUST BE CAREFUL. MY WHOLE LIFE IS ON THIS THING.
RELAX.

NOT ONE FEATHER ON A SINGLE ANGRY BIRD WILL BE HARMED.
YOU HEAR THAT, GUYS?

OKAY, IPHONE, YOU'RE SMART ENOUGH TO RUN MY LIFE. LET'S GET STARTED.
Okay.

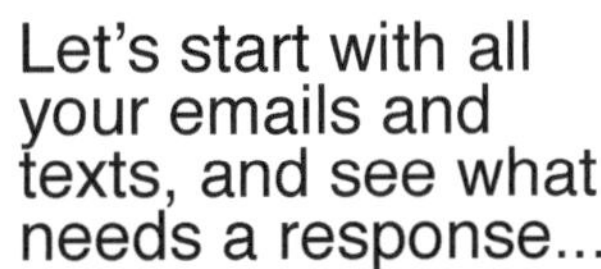
Let's start with all your emails and texts, and see what needs a response...

Almost done...

Twitter photo from Congressman. Open it?
DELETE! ALWAYS DELETE!

Sherman, your records indicate you're past due for a physical.
UGH.

Shall I make an appointment for you?
I HATE GOING TO THE DOCTOR.

If you like, I could go for you.
COULD YOU?

All of Sherman's vitals can be accessed through my microport.
I'M GETTING A GLOVE.

SO, YOUR IPHONE RUNS YOUR LIFE NOW?
DECISIONS, APPOINTMENTS, EVERYTHING.

THAT'S A LITTLE STRANGE.

What's strange is how **this** knucklehead got a gorgeous wife like **you**.
OH, MY.

WE SHOULD TALK.
Call me.

SHOW ME THIS NEW SOFTWARE THAT ERNEST CREATED FOR YOUR IPHONE.

IT'S AWESOME. NOW MY IPHONE PRACTICALLY LIVES MY LIFE FOR ME. CHECK IT OUT.

I recommend a five iron, sir.
GO AHEAD, IPHONE. TAKE THE SHOT FOR ME.
Yes, sir.

WHOA! THAT'S THE BEST SHOT YOU'VE HIT ALL DAY!
THIS'LL FREE ME UP TO FOCUS ON YOUR CHEATING.
WHACK!

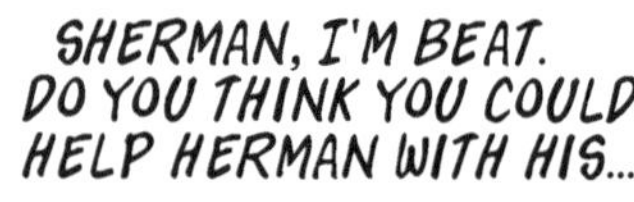
SHERMAN, I'M BEAT. DO YOU THINK YOU COULD HELP HERMAN WITH HIS...

Done.
MUNCH MUNCH

I already helped him with his homework, read him a story, and put him to bed.

THANK YOU, IPHONE. YOU THINK OF EVERYTHING.

WHAT IS IT WE NEED YOU AROUND HERE FOR AGAIN?
EYE CANDY.

SHERMAN'S LAGOON

HELLO. HOW'S EVERYONE DOING TODAY?

HELLO?

IS ANYBODY LISTENING?

I SEE... WE'RE ALL TOO BUSY "COMMUNICATING."

SO, THIS IS WHAT IT'S LIKE TO LIVE IN THE "INFORMATION AGE."

WHOO HOO! GOT AN EMAIL!

IT'S FROM POTTERY BARN!
SAY "HI" FOR ME.

SO, WHAT KIND OF MOVIE DO YOU RECOMMEND TONIGHT, IPHONE?

Forget the movie. why don't you and I hit a nightclub?
I BEG YOUR PARDON!

who do you love more? sherman or me?
I HATE TOUGH DECISIONS...

I'M GOING TO PUNT.
AAUUUGH!!
PUNT!

ERNEST, THERE'S SOMETHING WRONG WITH THE SOFTWARE YOU INSTALLED IN MY IPHONE.

NOW MY PHONE IS ACTING RUDE AND OBNOXIOUS. IT MADE A PASS AT MY WIFE. IT'S TURNED INTO AN OUTRIGHT PRIMA DONNA.

I'VE SEEN THIS PROBLEM BEFORE.

THE TECHNICAL TERM FOR IT IS "SHEENING."
I'm dealing with fools and trolls!

HELLO, MEGAN?
YES. DO I KNOW YOU?

CARRIE SHARPFIN, FROM LAGOON LIFE MAGAZINE.
OH, I LOVE THAT ONE!

WE'D LIKE TO PROFILE YOU AND YOUR HUSBAND IN AN UPCOMING ISSUE.

WHAT? GET THE @#$% OUT OF HERE!
AND... SHUTTING RECORDER OFF.

LAGOON LIFE MAGAZINE WANTS TO DO A PROFILE ON ME?
WELL...

YOU AND YOUR HUSBAND TOGETHER. CAN'T FORGET YOUR BETTER HALF.

WHAT IF I'M BOTH GOOD HALVES?
THAT'S WHAT EDITING IS FOR.

SHERMAN, I'D LIKE YOU TO MEET CARRIE SHARPFIN. SHE'S A JOURNALIST.
HELLO.
HI.

CARRIE'S MAGAZINE WANTS TO RUN A PROFILE ON US.
GET OUT!

IS THIS A PRANK? ARE WE ON CANDID CAMERA OR SOMETHING?

ALRIGHT, LADY! WHERE'S THE HIDDEN CAMERA! I WON'T BE MADE A FOOL!
TOO LATE.

MY FIRST QUESTION FOR THE ARTICLE WOULD BE...

HOW LONG HAVE YOU TWO BEEN A COUPLE?
SHERMAN?
GOSH, WE'VE BEEN TOGETHER SINCE WAY BACK WHEN.

COULD YOU BE MORE SPECIFIC?
A LONG TIME.

I MEAN, IN YEARS.
SHARK YEARS? DOG YEARS?
HE DOESN'T KNOW! ALRIGHT?

Sherman's Lagoon

SHERMAN, DO YOU EVER GET THE FEELING THAT THIS ISN'T THE FIRST TIME WE'VE BEEN MARRIED?

AT TIMES IT HAS SEEMED LONGER THAN A SINGLE LIFETIME.

MAYBE AT DIFFERENT POINTS IN THE TIME-SPACE CONTINUUM WE KEEP FINDING EACH OTHER.

ISN'T THAT ROMANTIC?

THE FORCES OF THE UNIVERSE HAVE CAST US TOGETHER OVER AND OVER FOR A REASON...

SO THAT WE EVENTUALLY FIND PERFECT LOVE.

SO, IF WE DON'T GET THIS RIGHT, WE COULD BE MARRIED AGAIN?
I'M AFRAID SO.

NEXT TOPIC FOR THE ARTICLE... KIDS.

WE HAVE A LITTLE BOY. HERMAN.

HIS SAFETY AND WELL BEING IS THE MOST IMPORTANT THING IN THE WORLD TO US.

CAN WE GET A PHOTO OF HIM FOR THE MAGAZINE?

WHERE'S HERMAN?
GOT ME.

OKAY, I THINK I HAVE EVERYTHING I NEED FOR THE ARTICLE.
GREAT.

IT'S BEEN AN HONOR TO INTERVIEW A COUPLE WITH SUCH A STRONG, LOVING BOND.

BYE-BYE.
CIAO.

COULD YOU HAVE EMBARRASSED ME ANY MORE?
HOW? I COULDN'T GET A WORD IN EDGEWISE!

IT'S HERE! OUR "LAGOON LIFE" MAGAZINE ARRIVED!

I CAN'T WAIT TO READ THE ARTICLE ON US.

OOH! THEY TALK ABOUT WHAT A WONDERFUL RELATIONSHIP WE HAVE.
LAGOON LIFE

THEY SAY WE COULD DO A "SEMINAR ON LOVE."
A LOVE SEMINAR, HUH?
LAGOON LIFE

HERE'S WHAT WE'LL NEED TO TURN A PROFIT...
WHERE'D **HE** COME FROM?
LAGOON LIFE

HERE YOU GO, FILLMORE.
WHAT'S THIS?
LOVE
SEMINAR

A BROCHURE ABOUT THE ONE-DAY LOVE SEMINAR THAT MEGAN AND I ARE DOING.
LOVE
Seminar

"HOW TO FIND RELATIONSHIPS, HOW TO HELP THEM GROW, HOW TO CULTIVATE THEM..."
LOVE

SOUNDS LIKE A SEMINAR ON GROWING MUSHROOMS.
"HOW TO TELL IF THEY'RE POISONOUS."
LOVE
Seminar

WELCOME TO OUR LOVE SEMINAR, EVERYONE.

TODAY, WE'RE GOING TO SHARE WITH YOU THE THINGS WE'VE LEARNED ON OUR CLIMB TO THE SUMMIT OF MARITAL BLISS.

EXCUSE ME, BUT DON'T YOU TWO FIGHT LIKE CATS AND DOGS?

HE MAKES A GOOD POINT.
THE REGISTRATION CLEARLY SAYS "NO Q&A"!!

LESSON ONE IN THE MEGAN AND SHERMAN LOVE SEMINAR...

COMMUNICATION IS THE KEYSTONE TO BUILDING A STRONG RELATIONSHIP.
communication

YOU NEED TO TALK. YOU MUST BE ON THE SAME PAGE AS YOUR MATE.
communication

I THOUGHT WE DECIDED "TRUST" WAS MOST IMPORTANT.
I DECIDED OTHERWISE.
communication

SHERMAN'S
LAGOON

SAYS HERE THAT "ONE SEA TURTLE YEAR EQUALS FIVE HERMIT CRAB YEARS."

I GUESS THAT MEANS YOU TURTLES LIVE FIVE TIMES LONGER THAN US CRABS.
'FRAID SO.

HMPH.

SO, THERE WILL COME A DAY WHEN...
YOU'LL BE GONE AND ANOTHER CRAB WILL TAKE YOUR PLACE. YEP.

AND THERE WILL BE ANOTHER CRAB AFTER THAT.

THERE WERE TWO OR THREE HERMIT CRABS BEFORE YOU...
THEY COME AND GO.

I LIKED THEM ALL.

ONCE YOU'RE GONE, I'LL LIKE YOU, TOO.
YOU'RE JUST SAYIN' THAT.

OKAY, EVERYONE, LET'S MOVE ON WITH OUR LOVE SEMINAR...
HOLD UP, MEGAN.
LOVE SEMINAR
WHAT IS LOVE?

HOW COME **YOU'RE** DOING ALL THE TALKING? WHEN IS IT MY TURN?

YOU GET TO TALK AFTER LUNCH. JUST PASS OUT THE SNACKS AND LET'S GET ON WITH IT.
FINE!

LITTLE CANDY HEARTS. HOW APPROPRIATE.
MINE SAYS "LOVE STINKS."

AND THAT CONCLUDES OUR SEMINAR ON LOVE.

WE HOPE OUR MARRIAGE HAS BEEN AN INSPIRATION TO YOU.

AND WE HOPE IT HAS, IN SOME WAY, GIVEN YOU INSIGHT ON HOW TO LEAD A HAPPIER LIFE.

I FEEL A LOT BETTER ABOUT BEING SINGLE.
ME TOO.

I'M GETTING THAT URGE.
URGE?

THE URGE TO START A NEW MONEY-MAKING VENTURE. IT'S TIME.

AND HOW EXACTLY CAN YOU TELL WHEN IT'S TIME?

THE LAWSUITS FROM MY PREVIOUS VENTURE HAVE ALL BEEN SETTLED.
GOTCHA.

HAVE YOU COME UP WITH AN IDEA FOR A NEW BUSINESS VENTURE YET?
NO...

AND IT'S DRIVING ME CRAZY! I'VE USUALLY GOT FIVE OR SIX BY NOW.

AM I LOSING MY MOJO? HAVE I LOST MY DRIVE?
NOT TO WORRY.

YOU'LL RIP OTHERS OFF AGAIN. IT'S WHO YOU ARE.
YOU REALLY THINK SO?

STILL BRAINSTORMING IDEAS FOR YOUR NEW BUSINESS VENTURE?
YEAH... NOTHING, SO FAR

MAYBE YOU NEED SOMEONE TO BOUNCE IDEAS OFF OF.
ARRRGHH!

WHACK!

HEY! IT WORKED!
DID I HEAR A "THANK YOU"?

I'VE GOT IT!
GOT WHAT?

A NEW IDEA FOR A BUSINESS VENTURE.
OH, JOY.

IT WAS RIGHT THERE IN FRONT OF ME. IT STRUCK ME WHILE I WAS EATING MY BREAKFAST CEREAL.

SO, WHAT IS IT?
A NEW BREAKFAST CEREAL.

SHERMAN'S LAGOON

ANGRY AGAIN, TODAY, ARE WE?
HMPH.

WHAT ARE YOU ANGRY ABOUT THIS TIME?
I HAVE NOT FOUND A REASON YET. I'M STILL LOOKING.

TRY BEING HAPPY.
I'M HAPPY.

HAPPY CAN BE CONTAGIOUS.

I BET IF YOU HANG AROUND ME LONG ENOUGH, MY HAPPY WILL WEAR OFF ON YOU, AND YOU'LL BE HAPPY, TOO.

HOW ARE YOU FEELING NOW?
I'M ANGRY THAT YOU'RE HAPPY.

SO, YOU'RE GOING TO MAKE YOUR OWN BREAKFAST CEREAL.
YEP.

EVERYONE EATS BREAKFAST! I CAN'T LOSE!
WHAT ARE YOU CALLING IT?

WELL, IT'S MADE MOSTLY OF SEAWEED, SO...
HMMMM...

WEEDIES!
CATCHY.

HOW GOES THINGS WITH YOUR NEW BREAKFAST CEREAL BUSINESS?
GOOD.
WEEDIES
Because Breakfast is good

"WEEDIES" WILL BE ON THE SHELVES IN NO TIME. MY R&D DEPARTMENT IS JUST TINKERING WITH THE FORMULA.

SHERMAN, HOW WAS THAT LAST BATCH?
UM.

STILL CAUSED A RASH, BUT NOT THE FACIAL NUMBING.
I'D BE OKAY WITH THAT.

HERE YOU GO, BOYS. THE CONTEST RULES.
WHAT CONTEST?

I'M PUTTING THE PICTURE OF A LOCAL HERO ON THE COVER OF MY "WEEDIES" CEREAL BOX.

CAN A "HERO" BE AN ARTIST OR A MUSICIAN?
SURE.

AS LONG AS SAID ARTIST OR MUSICIAN BATS OVER .300 OR CAN DUNK.
GOTCHA.

HAWTHORNE, REGARDING WHO YOU PUT ON THE "WEEDIES" CEREAL BOX COVER...
YES?
WEEDIES
Because Breakfast is good

I STRONGLY URGE YOU TO FEATURE A POET.
A POET?

THINK WHAT A GREAT MESSAGE THAT WOULD SEND TO OUR YOUTH ABOUT WHO OUR REAL HEROS ARE.
WEEDIES
Because Breakfast is good

DOES IT HAVE TO BE YOU, OR CAN IT BE A GOOD POET?
WELL, I NEVER THOUGHT YOU'D... HEY!

HAWTHORNE, ABOUT YOUR WEEDIES CEREAL BOX COVER...
HERE WE GO AGAIN.
WEEDIES
Because Breakfast is good

I HOPE YOU'RE CONSIDERING PUTTING A FEMALE ON IT.
WELL, I HADN'T...

OF COURSE, IT WOULDN'T BE UNPRECEDENTED. WHEATIES DID ONCE PUT MARY LOU RETTON ON THEIRS.
WEEDIES

DIDN'T YOU TRY TO BITE HER ONCE?
PERKY DOESN'T SIT WELL WITH ME.
WEEDIES

LET'S GO. HAWTHORNE'S ABOUT TO REVEAL WHO MADE THE "WEEDIES" CEREAL BOX COVER.

WELCOME, EVERYONE, TO MY BIG PRODUCT LAUNCH. SO, WITHOUT ANY FURTHER ADO...

TA-DAH!!
IT'S YOU!
BOO!
RIGGED!
WEEDIES

SO, HOW MANY BOXES CAN I PUT YOU DOWN FOR?
I SHALL BE STICKING WITH COUNT CHOCULA. A TRUE FRIEND.

LOOKS LIKE THAT GUY IS FINALLY GOING FOR A SWIM.

FINALLY! I'VE BEEN WAITING HOURS FOR THIS.

AND NOW YOU'RE GOING TO EAT HIM?
YEP. TODAY'S JUST NOT HIS LUCKY DAY.

DO YOU REALIZE THAT GUY HAS A GREATER CHANCE OF GETTING STRUCK BY LIGHTNING THAN EATEN BY A SHARK?

HE'S ABOUT TO BECOME A STATISTICAL ANOMALY...
COME TO PAPA.

HE'S ABOUT TO BECOME ONE OF THOSE EXTREMELY RARE PEOPLE WHO GET EATEN BY A SHARK.

CRACK!

UNLESS HE GETS STRUCK BY LIGHTNING FIRST.
NOT AGAIN!

OOH! A SUNKEN SHIP!
YEP.

SHOULD WE CHECK IT OUT?
I DUNNO.

YOU THINK AFTER ALL THIS TIME THERE'S STILL TREASURE INSIDE?

I WAS HOPING FOR A BATHROOM.
BE MY GUEST.

WHADDAYA SAY WE EXPLORE THIS OLD SUNKEN PIRATE SHIP?

PIRATE SHIP? WHAT MAKES YOU THINK THIS WAS A PIRATE SHIP?

THE CANNONS, THE DARK COLOR, THE SLEEK DESIGN...

THE BUMPER STICKER.
RIGHT.
How's My Looting?
Call 800-555-2020

SHERMAN, I THOUGHT I HEARD SOMETHING UP AHEAD.
FILLMORE, YOU'RE JUST IMAGINING THINGS.

THERE'S NOTHING IN THIS OLD SUNKEN PIRATE SHIP BUT RUSTY CANNONS AND ROTTED PLANKS.

BAAAA!

AND THIS GHOST THAT FORGOT HIS LINE.
DANGIT! IT'S "BOO," RIGHT?

HI, WHO ARE YOU?
I'M A GHOST. I SAILED WITH BLACKBEARD, THE PIRATE.

ARE YE FRIGHTENED?
YOU DON'T SEEM THAT SCARY TO ME.

MY NAME'S WILLIE. I WAS THE SHIP'S ACCOUNTANT. I CAN'T SEEM TO FRIGHTEN ANYONE.

MATH FRIGHTENS ME.
ARGH, YOU'RE JUST SAYIN' THAT.

WILLIE, WHAT WAS IT LIKE SAILING WITH BLACKBEARD?

EVERYONE WANTS TO KNOW ABOUT BLACKBEARD!
UH, SORE SPOT?

NOBODY WANTS TO HEAR A STORY ABOUT THE HIGH SEAS ADVENTURES OF WILLIE, THE PIRATE ACCOUNTANT.

THERE WE WERE, MILES FROM SHORE, AND I NEEDED AN OFFICE DEPOT...
LOOKS LIKE WE'RE GOING TO HEAR ONE.

SO, WILLIE, DO YOU WISH YOU WERE A SCARY GHOST?
AYE. OF COURSE.

BUT, HOW SCARY CAN THE GHOST OF A PIRATE ACCOUNTANT BE?

WHAT'S THE SCARIEST GHOST LINE YOU GOT?
HMMM...

OOOOH, THAT DEDUCTION COULD BE A RED FLAG FOR THE I.R.S.!
NON-ACCOUNTANT SCARIEST LINE.

SHERMAN'S LAGOON

WHY CAN'T EVERYONE JUST GET ALONG?

NOT EVERYONE SEES THINGS THE SAME WAY.
AND WHEN THAT HAPPENS, SOMETIMES THEY DON'T GET ALONG.

LIKE YOUR COLOGNE.
HUH?

TO YOU, IT'S FRAGRANT AND SUBLIME. TO ME, IT'S BILGE WATER.
NICE EXAMPLE.

OR YOUR HEADBANGER MUSIC COLLECTION. YOU HEAR MUSIC, YET I HEAR MONKEYS BEING TORTURED.
TOUCHÉ.

YOU SEE? THAT'S CALLED "GETTING ALONG."
NOT EVERYBODY CAN DO IT.

OR THIS BRICK. YOU FEEL PAIN, YET I FEEL PLEASURE.
OW!
GOOD ONE.

WILLIE, I SENSE YOUR FRUSTRATION. YOU'RE THE GHOST OF A PIRATE, BUT NOBODY SEEMS TO BE AFRAID OF YOU.

AYE. WHENEVER ANYONE SEES A GHOST PIRATE, THEY THINK "PIRATES OF THE CARIBBEAN."

THEY THINK I'M SOME HOLOGRAPHIC PROJECTION - AN AD FOR THE NEXT MOVIE.

I HATE DISNEY.
SHHH! THEY'RE LISTENING. THEY'RE ALWAYS LISTENING.

HEY, WILLIE, MAYBE MY FRIEND HAWTHORNE CAN HELP...
HAWTHORNE, THIS IS WILLIE.
HI.

WILLIE'S A PIRATE GHOST, BUT NOBODY IS AFRAID OF HIM.
I SEE.

LET'S MAKE SOME WARDROBE CHANGES... EYEPATCH... PEG LEG... HOOK... THAT'S IT.

I FEEL SO CLICHÉ.
AND NOW A QUICK CHECK ON CRAIG'S LIST FOR DEAD PARROTS.

OKAY, WILLIE, ARE YOU READY TO CONTINUE YOUR IMAGE MAKEOVER?
NAH.

I'M JUST NOT CUT OUT TO BE A SCARY GHOST PIRATE.

AS A MATTER OF FACT, I'M TIRED OF BEING A RESTLESS SOUL. I THINK I'LL LAY LOW FOR A COUPLE HUNDRED YEARS...

... OR UNTIL THE ECONOMY IMPROVES.
WHICHEVER COMES FIRST.

I HEARD YOU'RE DOING AUDITIONS FOR A PRODUCTION OF "WIZARD OF OZ."
YEP.
Lagoon Community Theatre

THAT'S ONE OF MY ALL-TIME FAVORITES.
GREAT.

I WAS BORN TO CAPTURE DOROTHY'S INNOCENT AND SWEET NATURE.

OR ELSE HEADS WILL ROLL.
UH, NO NEED TO LOOK ANY FURTHER.

SO, YOU WEREN'T KIDDING ABOUT PUTTING ON ANOTHER SHOW.
NOPE.
Lagoon Community Theatre

AND I THINK IF WE ALL PULL TOGETHER...
Lagoon Community

WE CAN PUT ON A SHOW AS GOOD AS LAST YEAR'S.

BOY, YOU ACTUALLY SET THE BAR UNDERGROUND.
I'LL PUT YOU DOWN FOR USHER.

THIS YEAR, WE'RE PUTTING ON "THE WIZARD OF OZ."
OOH!

WILL THERE BE A MEATY ROLE IN IT FOR ME?
HERE YOU GO.

THIRD MUNCHKIN? BUT I'M HUGE AND DAUNTING. THIS WON'T WORK AT ALL!

CAN I MAKE HIM THE MUNCHBACK OF NOTRE DAME?
NO AD-LIBBING!

SHERMAN'S LAGOON

HEY, WANNA HIT THE LINKS? IT'S A BEAUTIFUL DAY.
CAN'T

MEGAN WENT OUT WITH THE GIRLS.

SO, HERMAN AND I ARE DOING A LITTLE FATHER-SON BONDING WHILE WE WATCH SOME GAMES.

PLUS, I'VE GOT ABOUT A HUNDRED ITEMS ON MY "HONEY DO" LIST.

I NOTICE YOU'RE NOT GETTING MANY OF THEM DONE.
I'M DOING ALL OF THEM WHILE I SIT HERE. I'M A VERY CLEVER SHARK.

LET ME SEE THAT!
HEY!
YANK!

"HONEY, DO NOT USE THE STOVE... HONEY, DO NOT TRY TO FIX ANYTHING...

HONEY, DO NOT PLAY WITH MATCHES."
ALRIGHT! YOU GET THE POINT!

TOP OF PAGE 22...
"TOTO... I'VE A FEELING WE'RE NOT IN KANSAS ANYMORE."
WOOF.

FILLMORE, ARE YOU PLAYING A ROLE IN "OZ"?
Lagoon Community Theatre

I SHALL BE PORTRAYING THE TIN WOODSMAN, WHO SADLY ROAMS THE FOREST WITHOUT A HEART.

OOOMF!
LEMME HELP YOU WITH THAT.

HEY, THIS THING IS PAPER MACHÉ.
MAYBE ASK OZ FOR BICEPS.

BRAVO, MEGAN!

THAT WAS A WONDERFUL RENDITION OF "SOMEWHERE OVER THE RAINBOW."

THERE ISN'T A DRY EYE IN THE HOUSE.

MAYBE BECAUSE A LOT OF SPIT FLIES WHEN YOU SING.
IT'S LIKE SEAWORLD. YOU SIT IN THE FRONT ROW, YOU SHOULD EXPECT TO GET WET.

WELL, I THOUGHT THE PLAY WENT WELL.
ARE YOU CRAZY?

YOU FORGOT ALL YOUR LINES! DOROTHY SQUIRTED OIL IN MY EYE! TOTO PEED ON THE TALKING TREES!

PLUS, THE AUDIENCE PELTED US WITH EGGS!

AND IN TODAY'S TOUGH ECONOMY, THAT'S SOMETHING.
I GOT HIT WITH A FOOD STAMP.

SHERMAN'S

HEY, SHERM, IS IT TRUE THAT MOST SHARKS HAVE TO KEEP MOVING OR THEY'LL DIE?
IT'S TRUE.

IF WE STOP MOVING. WE CAN'T BREATHE.

THAT'S ONE OF THE DOWNSIDES OF MY NICE NEW LOUNGE CHAIR.

IT IS VERY COMFORTABLE...

BUT I AM SLOWLY SUFFOCATING...

BUT IT IS VERY COMFORTABLE...

BUT, AT SOME POINT, THE SUFFOCATION WILL BECOME UNBEARABLE.

THAT'S WHEN I TURN ON THE BACK MASSAGER.
YOU'RE A VERY LAZY SHARK.

GOING SOMEWHERE, FILLMORE?
COCOS ISLAND, TO SPEND THANKSGIVING WITH FAMILY.

I SEE YOU'RE BRINGING THE STANDARD SEA TURTLE HOUSE GIFT.
YEP. A JAR OF PICKLED JELLYFISH.

EVERYONE'S GOTTEN ONE OF THOSE FROM YOU AT ONE TIME OR ANOTHER.

I HOPE YOU ENJOYED YOURS.
I MADE MINE INTO A LAMP.

HOW ARE YOU GETTING TO COCOS ISLAND, FILLMORE?
I'M CATCHING THE EQUATORIAL COUNTER CURRENT.

IT FLOWS RIGHT BY HERE, AND TAKES YOU ALL THE WAY TO CENTRAL AMERICA.
Equatorial Counter Current

NONSTOP? WOW!

DO THEY CHARGE FOR LUGGAGE?
YOU'RE ALLOWED ONE CARRY-ON.

BOY, THIS CURRENT IS PRETTY STR...
WHOOOAA!
Equatorial

LOOKS LIKE I'M COMING TO COCOS ISLAND WITH YOU, FILLMORE.

UH OH! YOUR SUITCASE GOT LEFT BEHIND!
GREAT...

INSTEAD OF LUGGAGE, I'M BRINGING BAGGAGE.
NOW YOUR BUTT'S ON FACEBOOK.

HERE WE ARE AT COCOS ISLAND. TIME TO PUT ON MY TRACKING DEVICE.
WELCOME TO COCOS ISLAND

WHAT'S THAT THING DO?
IT ALLOWS PEOPLE ALL OVER THE WORLD TO TRACK ME ON THE WEB.

WHY?
SO THEY CAN FOLLOW MY WILD AND CRAZY MEANDERINGS IN REAL TIME.

BUT YOUR REAL TIME IS SLOW MOTION.
YOU'RE JUST JEALOUS.
Follow Fillmore's track at http://seaturtles.org/fillmore

HERE WE ARE ON BAJO ALCYONE REEF. THIS IS WHERE THE HAMMERHEAD SHARKS HANG OUT.

THEY COME FROM ALL OVER TO GET CLEANED BY BARBERFISH.

IF PERSONAL HYGIENE WAS ALWAYS THIS FUN, I'D DO IT EVERY DAY.
Follow Fillmore's track at http://seaturtles.org/fillmore

COCOS ISLAND HAS SOME OF THE MOST BEAUTIFUL CORAL REEFS IN THE WORLD.

THAT'S BECAUSE THE WATERS AROUND HERE WERE DECLARED OFF-LIMITS TO FISHING.

PUTT PUTT PUTT

SO, ALL THE MEN FLOATING AROUND IN BOATS...
CAN'T FISH. THEY JUST DRINK BEER.
Follow Fillmore's track at http://seaturtles.org/fillmore

SHERMAN'S LAGOON

YOU WANTED TO SHOW ME SOMETHING?
MY NEW SMART KITCHEN. CHECK IT OUT.

JUST TELL THE SMART COFFEE MAKER WHAT YOU WANT.
REALLY? OKAY... ONE COFFEE. BLACK.

UH OH. THE SMART TOASTER MUST'VE OVERHEARD YOU. IT'S MAKING BLACK TOAST.

QUICK! YOU TALK TO THE COFFEE MAKER WHILE I TALK TO THE TOASTER.

REBOOT! REBOOT! START! RUN!
CANCEL! CANCEL! CONTROL ALT DELETE!

BEEP
BEEP
BRRRRZZT!
WHOOSH!
ZING!

ALL THIS SMART TECHNOLOGY WILL TAKE SOME GETTING USED TO.

YOUR SMART CAR JUST DROVE AWAY.
HEY!

HERE ON THE BAJO ALCYONE REEF YOU CAN SEE ALL KINDS OF THINGS...

SUCH AS THE RARE AND SPECTACULAR OCTOPUS MATING RITUAL.
Follow Fillmore's track at http://seaturtles.org/fillmore

SHE'S WATCHING "DANCING WITH THE STARS," AND HE'S ASLEEP ON THE COUCH.
IT DID SAY "RARE."

HERE'S ANOTHER FAMOUS COCOS ISLAND LANDMARK- DIRTY ROCK...
DIRTY ROCK?

IN SPANISH, IT'S CALLED "ROCA SUCIA."
SOUNDS BETTER IN SPANISH.

SO NAMED BECAUSE OF THE GENEROUS QUANTITIES OF "CACA DE PAJARO" FOUND THERE.
OOOH! WHAT'S "CACA DE PAJARO"?

BIRD POOP.
SOUNDS BETTER IN SPANISH.
Follow Fillmore's track at http://seaturtles.org/fillmore

THERE'S A LOCAL COCOS ISLAND SEA TURTLE. AND IT'S A SHE TURTLE.
I NOTICED.

WELL? AREN'T YOU GOING TO GO INTRODUCE YOURSELF?
MY SPANISH IS HORRIBLE.

ISN'T THERE A TURTLE LANGUAGE?
YES, BUT IT'S VERY LIMITED.

ALTHOUGH, WE DO HAVE OVER 100 WORDS FOR "JELLYFISH."
FASCINATING.
Follow Fillmore's track at http://seaturtles.org/fillmore

HOLA, SENORITA... UHHH... ¿CÓMO ESTÁ?
IT'S OKAY. I SPEAK ENGLISH.

MY NAME'S CARMEN.
CARMEN... WOULD YOU BE MY COUSIN, CARMEN, PERCHANCE?

IF WE'RE COUSINS, THAT WOULD PREVENT ME FROM ASKING YOU OUT.

BUT IF WE'RE NOT COUSINS...
THEN I'D HAVE TO SHOOT YOU DOWN.
Follow Fillmore's track at http://seaturtles.org/fillmore

SO, YOU'RE MY LONG-LOST COUSIN, CARMEN!
AND YOU'RE FILLMORE.

WE'RE FAMILY! WHO'D'VE THOUGHT MY FAMILY COULD BE SO ATTRACTIVE!
THANKS...

I GUESS YOU'RE SAFE TO HUG NOW.
SADLY, YES.
Follow Fillmore's track at http://seaturtles.org/fillmore

CARMEN, I WANT YOU TO MEET MY FRIEND, SHERMAN.
HI.

YOU'RE FRIENDS WITH A GREAT WHITE SHARK?
DON'T WORRY ABOUT HIM. HE'S HARMLESS.

GULP

HE'S CIRCLING ME.
HE'S JUST CHECKING FOR OPEN WOUNDS. NOT TO WORRY.
Follow Fillmore's track at http://seaturtles.org/fillmore

SHERMAN'S LAGOON

OH WISE TURTLE, WOULD YOU SAY THAT LIFE IS A MERITOCRACY?
NO... LIFE'S NOT FAIR LIKE THAT.

DO WE LIVE IN A SHARKOCRACY?
NO. THE WORLD'S NOT FAIR FOR SHARKS EITHER.

IS IT A TURTLEOCRACY?
DEFINITELY NOT.

SO, LIFE IS A CRABOCRACY.
HE'S THE ONLY ONE WHO ALWAYS SEEMS TO COME OUT ON TOP.

YOU DON'T GET IT.

THE WORLD BELONGS TO THOSE WHO KNOW WHAT THEY WANT AND ARE WILLING TO STEP ON OTHERS TO GET IT.

SO, LIFE'S A JERKOCRACY.
NO, IT'S NOT THAT BAD.

THIS IS THE ISLA MANUELITA CORAL GARDEN.
WOW.

AS YOU CAN SEE, IT'S A POPULAR SEA TURTLE HANG-OUT.

OF COURSE, WHEN YOU PUT THIS MANY TURTLES TOGETHER, YOU'RE ASKING FOR TROUBLE.

IT'S JUST TOO BIG TO BE ONE BOOK CLUB.
YOU HAVE TO BREAK THEM UP.
Follow Fillmore's track at http://seaturtles.org/fillmore

WELL, CARMEN, IT'S TIME FOR ME TO HEAD BACK HOME. IT'S VERY NICE TO HAVE MET YOU.

AND THANKS FOR SHOWING ME AROUND COCOS ISLAND. YOUR HOME IS VERY BEAUTIFUL...

A KISS RIGHT NOW WOULD BE NICE, BUT I GUESS THAT'S PRETTY MUCH IMPOSSIBLE.

OUR ENORMOUS NOSES WOULD GET IN THE WAY.
HUG.
Follow Fillmore's track at http://seaturtles.org/fillmore

OH, SHERMAN, YOU'RE BACK FROM COCOS ISLAND... AND JUST AS I WAS LEAVING.

WHERE ARE YOU GOING?
A CONVENTION.

SO, YOU'RE GIVING IT ALL UP AND JOINING A CONVENTION, HUH? I HAD NO IDEA YOU WERE SO RELIGIOUS.

YOU'RE THINKING OF A CONVENT, YOU BIG STUPID FISH!
THANK YOU FOR CORRECTING ME, SISTER.

SO, WHAT'S THIS CONVENTION YOU'RE GOING TO?

YOU WOULDN'T UNDERSTAND.

BECAUSE I'M DUMB?
BECAUSE I'M NOT BUSINESS SAVVY?
BECAUSE I'M NOT AS COOL AS YOU?

ARE YOU GOING TO CHOOSE ONE, OR DO I HAVE TO?
OKAY, I'LL GO WITH NUMBER TWO.

MEGAN, CAN I GO TO A CONVENTION WITH HAWTHORNE?

SHERMAN, I DON'T EVEN LIKE YOU GOING GOLFING WITH HAWTHORNE.

HE'S RUDE, CRUDE, MORALLY CHALLENGED, AND ALTOGETHER A BAD INFLUENCE.

HE'S ALSO STANDING RIGHT HERE.
I KNOW.

AHHH! THE ENTREPRENEURS CONVENTION!
WOW!

EVERY NEW TECHNOLOGY AVAILABLE TO MAKE YOUR HOME OFFICE EXPERIENCE COMPLETE.
Wireless Printing

SO, WHERE TO FIRST?

LET'S CHECK OUT THE GUMBALL MACHINES.
COOL.

SHERMAN'S LAGOON

IT'S A VERY NICE PAINTING.

YOU'RE JUST BEING POLITE.
NO. I REALLY DO LIKE IT.

YOU'RE JUST PRETENDING TO LIKE IT TO MAKE ME FEEL GOOD.

WHATEVER.

THAT'S GOT TO BE THE WORST PAINTING I'VE EVER SEEN. MY 5-YEAR-OLD NEPHEW CAN DO BETTER.

YOU'RE JUST BEING RUDE.
NO. I REALLY DO HATE IT.

FILLMORE, **YOU'RE** HERE AT THE ENTREPRENEUR'S CONVENTION?
I LOVE A GOOD TRADE SHOW.

FINDING ANYTHING COOL?
YEAH.

MY SHELL, ALTHOUGH A CLASSIC, WAS NEVER WIRED FOR ALL OF TODAY'S NEEDS... BUT NOW...

TA-DAH! STATE-OF-THE-ART POWER STRIP.
HAVE YOU JUST COMPLETELY GIVEN UP ON DATING?

THIS ENTREPRENEUR CONVENTION IS MASSIVE.
OOH! CHECK THIS OUT!

THE COPYKING 3000!
GIVE IT A WHIRL.

IT COPIES, COLLATES, STAPLES AND FOLDS...
WOW. THAT'S A PRETTY FANCY FOLDING JOB.

YEP. THEN IT FLIES ITSELF WHERE IT NEEDS TO GO.
SWEET.

I'M GOING TO ENTER THE "ELEVATOR PITCH CONTEST." WISH ME LUCK.

WHAT ON EARTH IS AN "ELEVATOR PITCH"?

IT'S A FAST-AND-FURIOUS BUSINESS PROPOSAL I GIVE YOU WHILE WE RIDE IN AN ELEVATOR TOGETHER.

BY THE END OF THE RIDE, YOU LIKE ME ENOUGH TO GIVE ME MONEY.
THERE ISN'T A BUILDING TALL ENOUGH.

IT'S THE LAST DAY OF THE CONVENTION. I THINK I'VE GOT JUST ABOUT EVERYONE'S BUSINESS CARD.

TIME TO SEPERATE THEM INTO "USEFUL" AND "USELESS."

IT'S THE LAST DAY OF THE CONVENTION... I GUESS I SHOULD EAT SOMEBODY.
HERE. EAT ONE OF THESE GUYS.

HOW'S THE STARGAZING GOING, FILLMORE?
NOTHING REMARKABLE TONIGHT.

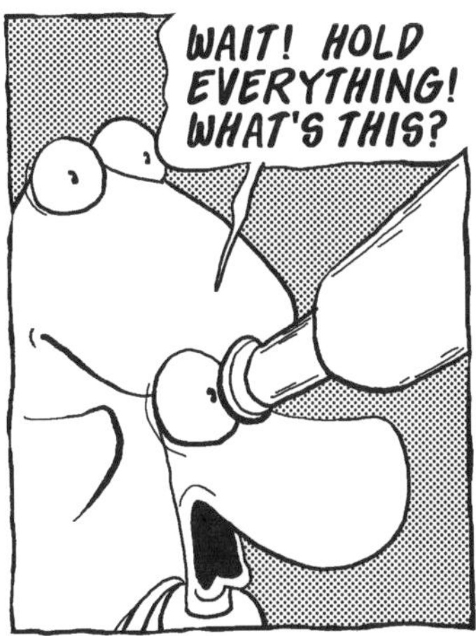
WAIT! HOLD EVERYTHING! WHAT'S THIS?

IT'S SOME KIND OF FIERY RED SPHERE! I'VE NEVER SEEN ANYTHING LIKE IT IN MY YEARS AS AMATEUR ASTRONOMER!

WHAT ARE WE LOOKING AT?
HAWTHORNE! MOVE!

I GOT SOMETHING HERE! THIS TIME IT'S FOR REAL!
REALLY?

I'LL HAVE TO CONFIRM IT, BUT IT APPEARS TO BE A PREVIOUSLY UNDISCOVERED METEOR!

SHERMAN, JOT DOWN THESE COORDINATES FOR ME! QUICK!
OKAY... HOLD ON...

DO YOU HAVE ANYTHING TO WRITE WITH BESIDES AN ETCH-A-SKETCH?!
JUST LET ME ERASE THESE STAIRS I WAS WORKING ON.

SHERMAN'S
LAGOON

I DON'T THINK YOU APPRECIATE THE ROLE CRABS PLAY IN THE ORDER OF THE UNIVERSE, DO YOU?

UMMM... SCAVENGER... BOTTOM FEEDER...
THAT'S A MERE DISGUISE.

WE ARE THE GREAT AND MYSTICAL REDISTRIBUTOR OF PAIN AND SUFFERING.

WE CHANNEL PAIN FROM THOSE WHO HAVE IT AND DON'T DESERVE IT...

...TO THOSE CAREFREE SOULS WHO MAKE NO CONTRIBUTION TO SOCIETY!

IT COMES IN THROUGH THE ANTENNAS AND OUT THROUGH THE CLAWS.

OW!

WAS THAT ONE OF YOUR MYSTICAL PAIN TRANSFERS?
NOPE. I JUST WANTED TO PINCH YOU.

YOU KNOW THAT GIANT METEOR I DISCOVERED LAST NIGHT?
YEAH?
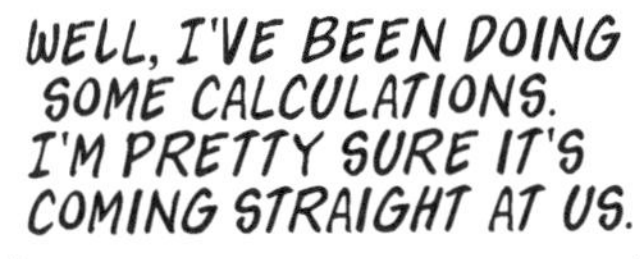
WELL, I'VE BEEN DOING SOME CALCULATIONS. I'M PRETTY SURE IT'S COMING STRAIGHT AT US.

THE END OF THE WORLD IS NIGH. IT'S JUDGEMENT DAY. WE'RE ALL GONNA DIE.

WHY COULDN'T YOU JUST DISCOVER A PUPPY OR SOMETHING?
I'M JUST THE MESSENGER!

HUMBLE CITIZENS OF KAPUPU LAGOON, I COME TO YOU BEARING GOOD NEWS AND BAD.

GIVE US THE GOOD NEWS FIRST.
I'VE DISCOVERED A METEOR, AND I'VE NAMED IT AFTER MYSELF.

WHAT'S THE BAD NEWS?
UM, IT'S GOING TO DESTROY THE EARTH.

WHAT'S THE LATEST IN SPORTS?
I'M STRICTLY NEWS.

SHERMAN, SINCE WE'RE ALL ABOUT TO BE WIPED OUT BY A METEOR, THERE'S SOMETHING YOU SHOULD KNOW.

I'VE HAD YOUR BLENDER, YOUR POKER CHIPS AND YOUR CIRCULAR SAW FOR OVER A YEAR.

I KNEW THAT.
OH...

DID YOU KNOW I SOLD THEM ON EBAY?
THAT PART'S NEW.

IF ARMAGEDDON IS TRULY APPROACHING, THEN I WANT TO DIE WITH NO REGRETS.

I'M FINALLY GOING TO ASK TANYA OUT ON A DATE.

I'VE GOT NOTHING TO LOSE, RIGHT?
GO FOR IT!
RIGHT!

SHOULD WE TELL HIM ABOUT THE T.P. HE'S GOT DANGLING FROM HIS SHELL?
IT CAN'T POSSIBLY MAKE ANY DIFFERENCE.

SHERMAN, NOW THAT THE END OF THE WORLD IS COMING, I'VE GIVEN SOME THOUGHT TO HOW I COULD'VE BEEN A BETTER WIFE...

I KNOW I PROBABLY TALKED TOO MUCH...
I SHOULD'VE LET YOU SPEAK FOR YOURSELF MORE...

I SHOULD'VE LET YOU COMPLETE YOUR OWN SENTENCES...
I SHOULD'VE LISTENED MORE...

ARE YOU GOING TO LET ME SAY SOMETHING BEFORE THE WORLD ENDS?
DON'T INTERRUPT.

METEOR IMPACT IS IN APPROXIMATELY 10 SECONDS!

I WANT US ALL TO SPEND THIS FINAL MOMENT TOGETHER IN HARMONY AND FELLOWSHIP.
LET'S HOLD HANDS, BROTHERS AND SISTERS.

PLOP!

WE'RE ALIVE!
YOU WON'T BE!
LET GO OF ME!

SHERMAN'S LAGOON
Season's Greetings

STILL HANDWRITING YOUR HOLIDAY CARDS? THAT'S SO 20TH CENTURY.

BELIEVE IT OR NOT, I ENJOY THIS ANNUAL RITUAL.
I USE A WEBSITE.

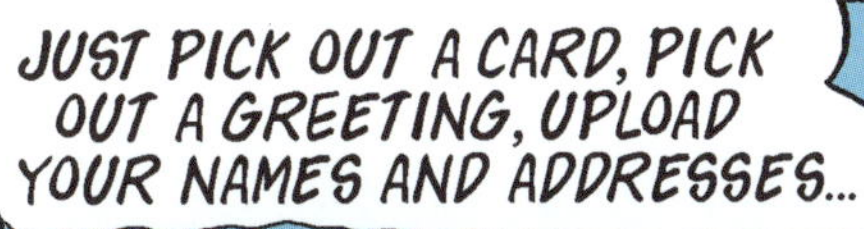
JUST PICK OUT A CARD, PICK OUT A GREETING, UPLOAD YOUR NAMES AND ADDRESSES...

...HIT A BUTTON, AND BOOM, YOU'RE DONE IN FIVE MINUTES.

I CHOOSE A NICE CARD; I USE A NICE PEN; I WRITE SOMETHING SPECIAL; I PUT TIME INTO IT.

YOU'RE NOT SAYING "SEASON'S GREETINGS."

YOU'RE SAYING, "YOU'RE ON MY DATABASE."

SEASON'S GREETINGS.
YOU'RE OFF MY DATABASE!!

HEY, FAT BOY! IS THAT A REMORA ON YOUR BACK?
YEP.

COOL! WILL YOU BE THE FIRST SHARK TO LET ME TRY MY NEW, PATENTED REMORA REMOVER?

WHY NOT?
BE RIGHT BACK!

WHAT IS IT? LIKE A SPRAY OR SOMETHING?
HOLD STILL.
NO! MOVE!

HE'S COMING! HE'S COMING!
QUIET ON THE PUTTING GREEN.

PERCY SNOTFIN, THE FAMOUS TRAVEL WRITER, IS GOING TO VISIT OUR LAGOON AND WRITE ABOUT IT!
SO?

AS MAYOR OF THIS PLACE, YOU NEED TO ROLL OUT THE RED CARPET!
SORRY. THIS YEAR'S ENTERTAINMENT BUDGET IS SPENT.

ARE THOSE NEW GOLF CLUBS?
OH, RIGHT. **AND** NEXT YEAR'S BUDGET.

MR. SNOTFIN! WELCOME TO KAPUPU LAGOON. THIS IS AN HONOR INDEED.

HELLO.

I'M FILLMORE, THE ONE WHO'S BEEN CORRESPONDING WITH YOU.
RIGHT.

I'M NOT SURE "CORRESPONDING" IS THE WAY I'D DESCRIBE IT.

THE ONE WHO'S BEEN STALKING YOU.
BETTER.

HAWTHORNE, THE TRAVEL WRITER FROM OCEAN LIFE MAGAZINE IS HERE.
SO?

HE PREFERS TO STAY IN LOCAL BED & BREAKFASTS.
GOOD FOR HIM.

WE DON'T HAVE ONE! WE NEED TO CONVERT YOUR CRAB HOLE INTO A BED & BREAKFAST IMMEDIATELY!
WELL...

HE GETS HIS OWN BED!
AS LONG AS HE DOESN'T MIND THAT I SLEEP IN THE BUFF.

HAWTHORNE, HAVE YOU TRANSFORMED YOUR PLACE INTO A QUAINT BED & BREAKFAST YET?
YEAH, YEAH.

DID YOU ADD TOUCHES OF CHARM, AND MAKE IT SEEM LIKE HOME?
JUST LIKE YOUR GRANDMA'S.

BRING YOUR SNOOTY TRAVEL WRITER IN.
OH, YOO HOO! MR. SNOTFIN!

YOU CAN SLEEP ON THE POKER TABLE. JUST SET THAT ONION DIP ON THE FLOOR.
OF COURSE.

GOOD MORNING, MR. SNOTFIN.
GOOD MORNING.

I TRUST YOU HAD A GOOD NIGHT'S REST AT OUR LOCAL BED & BREAKFAST.

SPLENDID. NOTHING BEATS A SLEEPER SOFA FOR COMFORT.

AND WHAT WERE THOSE CHARMING LOCAL PASTRIES YOU SERVED FOR BREAKFAST?
POP TARTS.

SHERMAN'S LAGOON

THERE'S ONE MORE PRESENT UNDER THE TREE. I DON'T KNOW WHO IT'S FOR.

THAT ONE'S FOR ME.

IT'S FROM YOU.
IT IS?

YEP. YOU ROMANTIC FOOL.

I SAW IT WHEN I WAS CHRISTMAS SHOPPING AND I JUST HAD TO HAVE IT.

A DIAMOND NECKLACE? OH! IT'S BEAUTIFUL!
AUGH!!

I'M SUPPOSED TO ACT SURPRISED AND YOU'RE SUPPOSED TO ACT NOT SURPRISED.
SORRY. LET'S TRY IT AGAIN.

SHERMAN, YOU'VE GOT TO HELP!
HUH? HOW?

THE TRAVEL WRITER WHO'S VISITING OUR LAGOON - HE WANTS TO SEE THE LOCAL WINERIES.
SO?

SO? WE DON'T **HAVE ANY LOCAL WINERIES!**
I NEED **YOU** TO POSE AS A VINEYARD OWNER.

I THOUGHT I WAS PLAYING THE PART OF THE LOCAL MUTE.
THINGS HAVE CHANGED!

MR. SNOTFIN, WELCOME TO LAGOON'S FARM WINERY.

WE OFFER TWENTY-ONE FLAVORS OF LAGOON'S FARM WINE...

...FROM STRAWBERRY TO WILD ISLAND MANGO WINE. WHAT FLAVOR WOULD YOU LIKE TO TRY?

DO YOU HAVE GRAPE?
GRAPE?
NO GRAPE.

HERE'S THE BIGGEST TOURIST ATTRACTION IN THE LAGOON, MR. SNOTFIN.

WE THINK IT'S PART OF A SPUTNIK.

TOURISTS COME FROM ALL OVER TO SEE THIS RELIC OF THE COLD WAR.
FASCINATING.

WE'RE PRETTY SURE IT'S RADIOACTIVE.
YOU CAN'T STAY LONG, YOU'LL GET TUMORS.